A Model for Life Success

An Introductory Leadership Development Program for anyone desiring to strengthen their ability to lead themselves and influence others.

This introductory Leadership Development program guide contains five chapters of leadership principles for success:

Chapter 1: LeaderSELF: A Model for Life Success,
Chapter 2: Principle #1-Self-Awareness (introspective focus),
Chapter 3: Principle #2-Self-Management (behavioral focus),
Chapter 4: Principle #3-Interacting with Others (interpersonal focus), and
Chapter 5: Principle #4-Influencing Others (team and organizational focus).

Participants will have an opportunity to understand these concepts and develop skills to contribute to the success experienced by themselves, their teams and the organization. An emphasis is placed on individual "real-time" activities which apply and reinforce the concepts.

LeaderSELF Resource Guide
©Copyright www.danduffyauthor.com

Introduction: Continuous Improvement=Breakthrough

Chapter One

LeaderSELF: A Model for Life Success

Welcome to leadership development! Whether you are an experienced leader or a newcomer to leadership, there is always something you can do to sharpen your skills, and that's what this leadership development program guide is all about. The purpose of this program is to assist you to learn, or perhaps reinforce leadership principles of success. We're going to cover the following four principles: #1: Self-Awareness (introspective focus), #2: Self-Management (behavioral focus), #3: Interacting with Others (interpersonal focus) and #4: Influencing Others (team and organizational focus). The program will be useful and informative for anyone who desires to enhance their leadership skills, regardless of whether or not they are currently in a leadership position or role. Whether you are new to your role, or are an experienced leader, it is anticipated that this develop-ment program will provide you with a fresh perspective.

It has been said that there is no such thing as an excellent organization, only those that believe in continuous improvement. We'd like to view this concept on an individual level, by suggesting that there is no such thing as the "perfect" leader, only those who believe in continuous improvement. Just think for a moment, each one of us has specific skills, abilities, resources and experiences. And, where we are now, in terms of what we are achieving, is the direct result of our past development, skills and commitment.

> **The Japanese describe it as "Kaizen" or Continuous Improvement**
> Making incremental improvements, doing "little things"
> better; setting and achieving ever higher standards of
> performance.

Skills + Activities=Performance

The idea of continuous improvement simply means that we can always learn to do some-thing better, more effectively, and the key to enhancing performance and obtaining results is for us to be...
- open,
- ready to learn,
- capable of sharing,
- willing to change and
- able to adapt how we conduct ourselves.

We are anticipating that this development program will provide you with the opportunity to identify your unique perspective, learn about and apply principles of leadership success. Your development initiative can be enhanced if you chose to experience the program with a friend or colleague. This approach will allow for you and your colleague to work together and share ideas, strengthening the learning process and creating a strong foundation to become the leader that you know you can be! So let's get started by exam-ining a formula for your developmental success......

Skills + Activities =Performance

This formula is quite simple. The **Skills** portion refers to the abilities, techniques and competencies that each one of us has as a leader. The **Activities** portion of the formula refers to your visible observable actions or practices in applying skills to your day-to-day challenges and responsibilities, at home, at work, and at play. And the **Performance** segment of the equation refers to the results that you, your team, and the organi-zation achieves.

What are some examples of skills that you currently have and activities which you currently demonstrate which significantly influence your performance?

- My Skills:_____
- My Activities:_____
- How satisfied are you with your current level of skills and activities and your performance? _____

LeaderSELF: A Formula for Success

LeaderSELF = Self-Awareness + Self-Management
Interacting with and Influencing Others

LeaderSELF is a model providing a strategy for recognizing, developing and demonstrating effective leadership. It contains four distinct, yet interconnected, emotional intelligence components:

a. Self-Awareness (introspective focus),
b. Self-Management (behavioral focus),
c. Interacting with Others (interpersonal focus), and
d. Influencing Others (team and organizational focus).

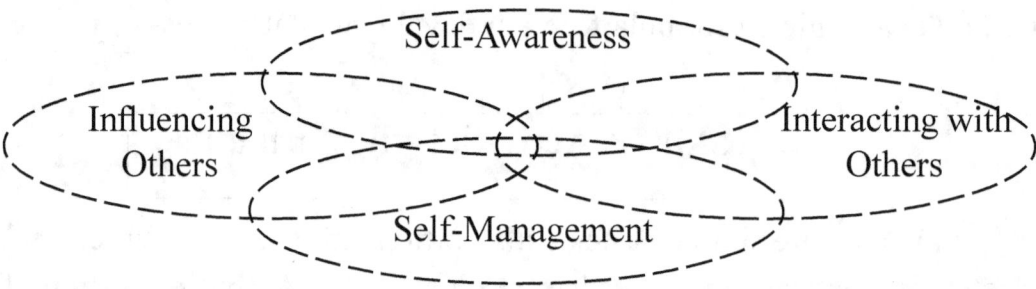

The LeaderSELF model emphasizes the interrelationship among each of the four components. In addition, the model displays the importance of developing competencies within each of the areas. As you strengthen your competencies, each of these areas become more "aligned," enhancing your Zone of Impact (the overlapping area).

These four components serve as hallmarks guiding you in your ability to:

- accurately self-assess your strengths and areas for improvement,
- understand and lead your "SELF,"
- communicate and manage interactions with others, and
- demonstrate influence within teams and the organization.

Understanding LeaderSELF Principles

Principle #1: Self-Awareness (introspective focus)
- **Knowing My Self**   "Where am I going?"
  - *My Interests: "What do I enjoy?"
  - *My Needs: "What do I need to work on?"
  - *My Values: "What is important to me?
  - *My Skills: "Do I know and apply LeaderSELF principles?"
  - *My Unique Qualities: "LeaderSELF Assessment Inventory"

Principle #2: Self-Management (behavioral focus)
- **Leading My Self**   "How do I demonstrate self-determination?"
  - *My Purpose: "What is my life focus?"
  - *Beliefs: "How do my beliefs influence my behavior?"
  - *Self-Talk: "How can purposeful self-talk transform my beliefs?"
  - *Motivation: "How can I be energized, directed, and sustained?"
  - *Goals: "What are my goals and how do I accomplish them?"

Principle #3: Interacting with Others (interpersonal focus)
- **Interpersonal Savvy:**   **"How do I strengthen my interactions with others?"**
  - *Acceptance/Trust: "How do I convey acceptance, respect, and trust?"
  - *Left-Brain/Right-Brain: "Understanding preferences improves my interactions."
  - *Communication Styles: "Identifying styles enhances my ability to communicate.
  - *Communication: "How do I improve my ability to speak, listen, and empathize with others?"
  - *Interacting with Impact: "How do I develop my ability to interact with others?"

Principle #4: Influencing Others (team and organizational focus)
- **Leading By Example:** "How do I take action on challenges/opportunities?"
  - *Shared Vision: "How do I inspire others through shared vision?"
  - *Developing Others: "How do I build team and organizational capacity?"
  - *Managing Conflict: "How do I de-escalate disagreements and strive for mutually agreeable resolutions."
  - *Guiding Change: "How do I initiate ideas and new directions."

The Four Principles of LeaderSELF:
Principle #1: Self-Awareness

The Four Principles of LeaderSELF

Your LeaderSELF profile can be summarized by four essential principles, each of which have to be examined, understood and demonstrated in order for you to be as effective as possible. These principles are: Self-Awareness, Self-Management, Interacting with Others, and Influencing Others. Let's define them individually and outline how the LeaderSELF Leadership Development Program will relate to each of the four principles.

Principle #1: Self-Awareness (introspective focus)
Greek Philosopher, Socrates taught eons ago that, "An unexamined life is not worth living." This personal and professional development program will provide you with an opportunity to "Know Thyself," through engaging in critical self-assessment, expanding self-knowledge and understanding. As you discover your unique qualities, you will heighten your self-concept. As you further gain insight through increased self-awareness, you will become more self-confident. The self-awareness aspect of your LeaderSELF analysis will focus on assessment of your interests, needs, values, and skills. These four self-awareness components impact your level of motivation and commitment, as

---

Self-Awareness Components

My Interests: When I am interested in something, I **LIKE** what I am doing.

My Needs: When it conforms to my needs, I am **SATISFIED**.

My Values: When it addresses my values, I am **FULFILLED**.

My Skills: When I am skilled at what I am doing, I meet with **SUCCESS**. These skills involve effective speaking, listening, and the ability to provide feedback.

By understanding my personal interests, needs, values, skills, and purpose, I can more effectively understand myself and others.

The Four Principles of LeaderSELF: Principle #2: Self-Management

Principle #2: Self-Management (behavioral focus) Highly effective indi-viduals understand that before they can manage or lead **others**, they must first manage and lead **themselves**. This is an important principle of LeaderSELF because it underscores essential characteristics and behaviors that must be mastered and become visibly apparent in your day-to-day behavior. By behavior, we mean, that you are demonstrat-ing specific characteristics through your visible observable actions. Your behavior is influenced by your beliefs. And, your beliefs and assumptions about yourself and those around you, influence and determine your perceptions of life.

My Purpose: Your potential and purpose represent your internal compass, guiding your life and career choices. Somewhere, deep inside you, you know what you want. It may take a little work to become aware of it, but it's there. And it is probably one of the most important issues in your life. You can't possibly get what you want unless you first *know* what you want.

My Beliefs, A Powerful Influence on Self and Others: My beliefs are the mental acceptance of or conviction in the truth or actuality of something. In essence, my BELIEFS are something that I don't know but ACCEPT as TRUE.

My Self-Talk/Affirmations: To affirm means "to make firm." An affirmation is a strong, positive statement that something is already so. It is a way of "making firm" that which you are imaging. It is a powerful technique, one which can in a short time transform many of your attitudes and expectations about life, and thereby help to change what you create for yourself.

My Motivation: The study of behavior and motivation is a search for answers to perplexing questions about human nature. Motivation deals with the choices you make, the energy you expend, and the channeling of your efforts. Motivation concerns incentives that induce you to increase your efforts toward some goal.

My Goals and Goal-Setting: When asked "what do you want," many people respond "I don't know." Well, if you don't know what you want, how do you know you don't already have it? And, if you don't know what you want, how will you know when you find it? What you want could be available to you and you wouldn't recognize it because you wouldn't know what it is.

The Four Principles of LeaderSELF:
Principle #3: Interacting with Others

Principle #3: Interacting with Others (interpersonal focus) Relationships at work, home and play are built upon respect and trust. Further, as human beings, we share one thing in common. We are all unique! Understanding the personal styles and preferences of yourself and others provides you with the ability to appreciate differences and adjust your style and preference to "match" that of another. As a result of this approach, you allow an individual to remain in their comfort zone. And when comfort levels increase, so does their ability to cooperate. Individuals who display the capability of relating well with others are said to have "interpersonal savvy," or the practical know-how of interacting with impact.

Demonstrate acceptance, respect, and trust, establishing rapport: Capable leaders realize the importance of demonstrating acceptance, respect and trust, supporting the self-confidence and self-esteem of others.

Are you Left-Brained or Right-Brained?: It is worthwhile to identify your abilities within the areas of rational, logical, and sequential "left-brain" and holistic, intitutive, and emotional "right-brain" oriented characteristics.

Understanding Personal Communication Styles: Determining your perspective of being direct or indirect and focused on people or task influences your preferences for interaction within the areas of communication, motivation, and teamwork.

Communication: Key elements of communication involve speaking, observing, hearing, and providing feedback. However, to communicate effectively you must also engage in an internal process of: listening (as a result of the other person speaking), interpreting (translating information which you "selected" through observing the speaker), and evaluating (giving meaning to your listening of the speaker's message.)

Interacting with Impact: If you make up your mind that it is impossible to get along with everybody...then you are halfway there to proving yourself correct. You won't get along with everybody! In fact, until you make up your mind that you can get along with everybody...there will always be somebody you will think is difficult, challenging or impossible to get along with. In order to interact with impact, you need to develop *behavioral flexibility*--the ability to adapt your behavior appropriately to meet the needs of the person with whom you are interacting.

The Four Principles of LeaderSELF: Principle #4: Influencing Others

Principle #4: Influencing Others (team and organizational focus)

Accomplished leaders concentrate on creating an organizational environment within which all people feel free to contribute, learn and excel, thereby providing them with a sense of purpose and fulfillment. This environment values communication, constituent leadership, and teamwork, focused on a shared vision of the future.

Creating a Non-Threatening Environment: Aim to build consensus through high levels of interaction, mutual exchange and collaboration, creating an environment neutralizing the potential for *power over* relationships.

Inspiring Shared Vision: Contemporary leaders recognize the need to facilitate a compelling shared vision projecting how the organization intends to grow through individual, team and organizational excellence.

Encouraging Constitutent Leadership: Because leadership is defined as a relation-ship, characteristics that can be attributed to *leaders* can also be used to describe the behavior of *constituents*. As such, the role of leader and constituent (follower) are in fact two sides of the same coin.

Developing Others through Empowerment, Delegation and Teamwork: Empowerment, delegation and teamwork are involved in accomplishing organizational purposes through the proper deployment of people. The aims of these approaches and *leadership* are similar: to accomplish organizational ends while enhancing the abilities, confidence, and initiative of constituents.

Managing Conflict: Focus on the specific situation, issue, or behavior (cool conflict), not on the person (hot conflict). By employing this practice, you build rapport and avoid defensive and uncooperative behavior. This approach is important to keep in mind, whether one is providing another with praise or criticism.

Guiding Change focused on Systematic Inquiry: A five-phase problem solving process permits organizations to establish a methodology promoting individual and/or organizational change through inquiry, interaction, and collaboration. The phases are:

1. Assessment, 2. Development, 3. Implementation, 4. Measurement/Monitoring and 5. Evaluation.

The Four Principles of LeaderSELF: A Summary and a Beginning

Now that you have a basic understanding of the four principles of LeaderSELF, think about both your skills and activities within each of the four areas and rate yourself on a Scale of 1 (I need improvement) to 5 (I am a role model):

SKILLS (The What)

Self-Awareness
1................2................3................4................5

Self-Management
1................2................3................4................5

Interacting with Others
1................2................3................4................5

Influencing Others
1................2................3................4................5

ACTIVITIES (The How)

Self-Awareness
1................2................3................4................5

Self-Management
1................2................3................4................5

Interacting with Others
1................2................3................4................5

Influencing Others
1................2................3................4................5

1. Which of the four principles do you think is most important to a leader?

2. Which of the four principles do you think is most important to an organization?

3. If you were to prioritize each of the above four principles from #1-4 in order of importance, what order would you put them in and why?

Leadership Definitions, Elements, and Observations

Definitions

"**Leadership is a process** by which groups, organizations and societies attempt to achieve common goals." The Leaders Companion

"**Leadership is an influence relationship...**
among leaders and their collaborators who intend real changes that reflect their mutual purposes." John Rost

"**Leadership is an influence relationship between two or more individuals focused on a common goal.**"
Dan Duffy and Don Doran

Elements

Effective Leaders...
- Challenge the Process
- Inspire a Shared Vision
- Model the Way
- Enable Others to Act
- Encourage the Heart

Kouzes & Posner

Effective Followers...
- Are critical to the success of leaders
- Manage themselves well
- Commit to organizational goals
- Show courage and honesty

Robert E. Kelley

Observations

Effective leaders develop competencies and traits within the following areas:

- thinking critically
- creating a vision
- creating change
- making decisions
- working on teams
- taking initiative
- gaining the capacity to develop people
- communicating
- resolving conflict
- solving problems
- acting with integrity
- valuing diversity
- acting with a sense of urgency

Let's Get Rid of Management

> People don't want to be managed.
> They want to be led.
> Whoever heard of a world manager?
> World leader, yes,
> Educational leader.
> Political leader.
> Scout leader.
> Labor leader.
> Business leader.
> They lead.
> They don't manage
> The carrot always wins over the stick.
> Ask your horse
> You can lead your horse to water,
> but you can't manage him to drink.
> If you want to manage somebody,
> Manage yourself.
> Do that well
> and you'll be ready
> to stop managing.
> And start leading.

Published in the Wall Street Journal by United Technologies

Individual Activity: Why would we want to get rid of management within organizations? Review the last few words of the above statement: "Manage yourself. Do that well and you'll be ready to stop managing and start leading." Take a few minutes to first, write down on a piece of paper words that come to mind relating to "Manager." Do the same for those words relating to "Leader." What is the "theme" or central idea within your words associated with "Manager" and "Leader?" After you have completed the above activity, turn to page 13 and review a comparison between "Management" and "Leadership." The above statement by United Technologies underscores today's need for leaders who are self-directed, motivational, and dynamic.

Management vs Leadership

MANAGEMENT	LEADERSHIP
*To Produce Order	*To Produce Change
*To Achieve Consistency	*To Achieve a Vision
*Planning	*Setting The Direction
*Coping With Complexity	*Coping With Change
*Organizing and Staffing	*Aligning People
*Independent Functions	*Interdependent Functions
*Controlling	*Motivating
*Other Directed	*Self Directed
*Reactive	*Proactive

> **Leaders not only manage people and resources, but potential.**

Page Summary: The left column depicts that management is about controlling people and resources to get done what the manager wants to accomplish. Whereas, the right column illustrates that leadership is about creating an environment within which people can contribute, excel and leave at the end of the day with a sense of fulfillment and purpose. It also describes mobilizing and aligning people and resources toward a shared vision. By creating an environment that inspires people to contribute and do their best, leaders are "awakening the gifts within" each individual. As individuals become aware of their "gifts" their potential for contribution is expanded.

Remember: It's not a question of leadership versus management. It's a recognition that leaders "lead people" and managers "manage things." Both approaches contribute to organizational success and one individual can exhibit both behaviors.

Leadership Questionnaire

Instructions: Please take a few minutes to read each statement about leadership and write your response in the space provided:

1. I feel the most important quality a leader can have is:
   _____

2. A person whose leadership capabilities I respect is:
   _____

3. Three things I admire most about this person are:
   _____
   _____
   _____

4. I feel my strongest leadership qualities are:
   _____
   _____

5. I would like to improve my leadership skills in the following areas: _____
   _____
   _____

6. On a scale of 1 (low) to 10 (high), I feel my rating as an effective leader is _____

Page Summary: According to Kouzes and Posner, who wrote <u>The Leadership Challenge,</u> effective leaders demonstrate: competence, forward-thinking, inspiration, and integrity. Effective leaders are also skilled communicators and team builders, accomplishing goals through teamwork. It is commendable that you have taken a risk to identify those areas about your skills that you would like to strengthen.

Keep in mind that developing your leadership effectiveness is a JOURNEY of CONTINUOUS IMPROVEMENT for everyone of us. The concept of continuous improvement also relates to how you rated yourself as a leader within item #6. Think of your current self rating as a baseline of information for tracking your future progress.

Enhancing Your Leadership Effectiveness is a Journey; Not a Destination!

Discovering Your Unique Qualities

Chapter Two

Principle #1: Self-Awareness (introspective focus)

> Personal growth and development begins with an introspective look at self...
> The process enables an individual to "awaken the gifts within."

The self-awareness aspect of the LeaderSELF framework emphasizes the importance of introspective assessment of your interests, needs, values, and skills. These four areas describe key components of your self, which when appraised, enhance self-understanding.

Interests: You like those things that interest you. You get enjoyment from your interests. In fact, you become more interesting to others in direct proportion to the depth and variety of your interests.

Needs: Psychologist, Abraham Maslow defined a "Hierarchy of Needs," ranging from physiological (food, shelter, clothing), to safety (security), to love and belonging (friendship, familty, intimacy), to esteem (self-esteem, confidence, respect) to self-actualization (attaining your highest potential). You have a sense of fulfillment when your needs are met.

Values: Your values are your internal compass that gives your life meaning and provides personal direction. You feel satisfaction when your values and actions are in alignment.

Skills: LeaderSELF skills are focused on specific qualities identified within each of the four principles. When you know your skills you are confident. Your confidence pre-pares you for future challenges. And, challenges are your opportunities for meeting with success.

Discovering Your Unique Qualities: Interests

Those things in your life that you have given special attention to comprise your interests. Your interests vary from activities such as: sports, computers, digital photography, "working out" at the fitness center, downloading and listening to music, travel, movies, volunteering, being with your friends, and many other undertakings.

Because interests are so varied, not all people share the same interests. As a result, it is important to first understand your own interests. By examining your interests, your awareness will be raised about those things that: appeal to you, arouse your attention, engage, intrigue, entertain, engross, and excite you. WOW! Interests can be a powerful means to energize you. Begin your self-examination process by identifying at least twelve activities that interest you:

1. _____
2. _____
3. _____
4. _____
5. _____
6. _____
7. _____
8. _____
9. _____
10. _____
11. _____
12. _____

Transfer six of your interests to the LeaderSELF Assessment Inventory on p. 21

As you can imagine, you could continue this activity by filling several blank pages with information about those things that interest you. Take a few moments to reflect on the following questions about your interests and their impact on leadership. This activity can be enhanced by meeting with a colleague and comparing answers to these same questions.

1. Why is it important for a leader to understand his/her interests?
2. What role do interests serve within leadership?
3. How do I identify interests of constituents within my organization?
4. How do I leverage constituent interests for the benefit of the organization?

Learning about your interests and those of constituents strengthens your ability to create an environment valuing the uniqueness of people.

Discovering Your Unique Qualities: Needs

Your needs address an important question: "What do I want to focus on and improve?" It is important to engage in assessing your needs because the process provides you with information about the way things are and the way you would like them to be. And, results provide you with a pathway guiding you from where you are to where you want to go. Use the following three step method to assess your needs:

Step #1: Perform a "GAP" Analysis between your "current situation" and your "desired situation." The difference or "gap" between your current situation and your desired situation will clarify "opportunities for improvement." Keep in mind that "closing the gap" may require several steps, accomplished over time. Use the space below to describe three of your "Current Situations," relating to work, career, family, profes-sional development, etc. Within the "Desired Situation" section, think about and describe how your three current situations might be modified or changed to more adequately represent your desired situation.

"Current Situation"

Current Situation #1: _____
Current Situation #2: _____
Current Situation #3: _____

"Desired Situation"

Desired Situation #1: _____
Desired Situation #2: _____
Desired Situation #3: _____

Step #2: Identify Your Top 3 Priorities for Closing the "Gap" between your current situation and your desired situation. Remember, if you attempt to "prioritize" too many things, you run the risk of losing sight of the "vital few" vs the "trivial many."

Priority #1: _____
Priority #2: _____
Priority #3: _____

Step #3: Identify Possible Goals and Create an Action Plan for Implementation
The information you identified in Step #2 will be used during the goals and action planning segment of Chapter Three, Principle #2: Self-Management page 40.

Discovering Your Unique Qualities: Values

Individual Values Assessment

The purpose of this exercise is to assist you in clarification of your values. Values constitute the nucleus of your beliefs. Essentially, your values determine what is meaningful, influencing your life's direction and purpose. Through an ongoing process of clarifying your values, you become more self-aware of "core" beliefs, assumptions, and attitudes. Outcomes of this process can dramatically influence your sense of purpose, fulfillment, and satisfaction in life.

Values Clarification Worksheet

Consider the values listed below. See descriptions for these values on page 19. Check the 10 values that are most important to you personally. Select those that most often guide your actions and decisions. For the 10 you checked, rank them in order of importance, with "1" being most important to you and "10" being least important to you. **Transfer your top three values to the LeaderSELF Assessment Inventory on page 21.**

____ Achievement	____ Friendships	____ Service
____ Advancement	____ Growth	____ Spirituality
____ Authority	____ Independence	____ Stability
____ Balance	____ Integrity	____ Teamwork
____ Community	____ Knowledge	____ Winning
____ Contribution	____ Loyalty	____ Family
____ Creativity	____ Money	____ Security
____ Country	____ Performance	____ Self-Actualization
____ Enjoyment	____ Power	____ Quality
____ Fame	____ Recognition	____ Freedom

NOTE: There are many other values that may influence you. Feel free to add a value that is important to you if you don't already see it on the list.

Adapted from P. Senge, <u>The Fifth Discipline Fieldbook.</u>

Discovering Your Unique Qualities: Value Definitions

Value Definitions

Achievement: Accomplishing my goals; being successful

Advancement: Assuming greater responsibility; moving up in the organization
Authority: Supervising others; coordinating activities, people, and resources
Balance: Balance school, work, family and leisure
Community: Committing and contributing to mutual goals; cooperating and sharing
Contribution: Making a contribution to society; doing something meaningful
Country: Loving and supporting the land of your birth or citizenship
Creativity: Being innovative and inventive; using my imagination
Enjoyment: Enjoying what I do; doing the things that interest me
Excitement: Being involved in exciting and stimulating things
Fame: Being famous or well known; achieving renown
Family: Having a family; spending time with family
Freedom: Being free; having political independence; having civil rights

Friendships: Having close friendships; spending time with people I like and trust **Growth:** Learning new things; growing and facing new challenges
Independence: Working independently; being on my own; being free of control
Integrity: Maintaining the highest ethical standards; being honest and truthful
Knowledge: Having knowledge and skill; being competent in my field

Loyalty: Being faithful to a person, ideal, cause or duty; demonstrating allegiance
Money: Being paid well for what I do; getting bonuses or raises

Performance: Successfully accomplishing tasks; meeting deadlines; doing well
Power: Having power and authority; being able to exercise influence and control **Quality:** Producing high-quality products/services; being proud of my work
Recognition: Being recognized and rewarded for my contributions **Security:** Being comfortable and feeling safety
Self-Actualization: Growing toward and attaining my highest potential
Service: Serving and satisfying others; giving time or effort to others
Spirituality: Connecting with nature, the universe or a greater being
Stability: Functioning in a stable, harmonious environment
Teamwork: Working together; belonging to a well-functioning team or group

Winning: Competing with others; knowing the thrill of victory; winning the contest

Adapted from P. Senge, The Fifth Discipline Fieldbook.

Discovering Your Unique Qualities: Skills and Knowledge

Competence means, according to the 10th Edition of the <u>Merriam-Webster's Collegiate Dictionary,</u> to have "the capacity to function or develop in a particular way" and to demonstrate "requisite or adequate ability or qualities." Essentially, your competence and your skills and knowledge are interrelated because your skills and knowledge serve as the foundation of your competence.

> Your **Skills** inform you about **"How to do something."**
> They can be transferred through teaching, practice and learning.

For example, your ability to use a computer and word processing software to create a resume may be one of your skills. Take a few moments to think about your skills and identify three of them below:

1. _____
2. _____
3. _____

> **Transfer your three skills to the LeaderSELF Assessment Inventory on p 22**

> Your **Knowledge** is comprised of **"What you know."** The **things you know** are your **factual knowledge** and your **experiential knowledge** is what you have **learned from your experience**.

For example, you have absorbed factual knowledge from your formal education. And, your awareness of your SELF in relation to others is part of your experiential knowledge. Take a few moments to think about your areas of knowledge and identify three of them below:

1. _____
2. _____
3. _____

> **Transfer your three areas of knowledge to the LeaderSELF Assessment Inventory on p 22**

Adapted from <u>First, Break</u> All the Rules, Buckingham & Coffman.

Discovering Your Unique Qualities: LeaderSELF Assessment Inventory

This **LeaderSELF Assessment Inventory (LAI)** is designed to stimulate thinking about LeaderSELF principles of self-awareness, self-management, interacting with others, and influencing others. It can serve as a "GAP" Analysis between your "current situation" and your "desired situation." The difference or "gap" between your current situation and your desired situation will clarify "opportunities for improvement." Once opportunities for improvement are clarified, the process can assist in facilitating your goals for development.

1. **Do Not Complete this Assessment Now.** As you continue to complete the LeaderSELF guide, you will be directed to transfer information from the specific activity to a section of the LeaderSELF Assessment Inventory.

2. **After you have completed all of the LeaderSELF guide**, you can review each section of the LeaderSELF Assessment Inventory and decide which areas you think you are doing OK within, which areas you should focus more on, and which areas you should focus less on. Make a check mark for each item in the appropriate place.

3. Go back over the whole list and circle the number of the **three priority activities** at which you would like to improve most at this time.

	OK	Want To Focus More	Want To Focus Less
MY INTERESTS (List 6 items from p 16)			
1. _____	___	___	___
2. _____	___	___	___
3. _____	___	___	___
4. _____	___	___	___
5. _____	___	___	___
6. _____	___	___	___
MY VALUES (List top 3 values from p18)			
1. _____	___	___	___
2. _____	___	___	___
3. _____	___	___	___

(More on Next Page)

Discovering Your Unique Qualities: LeaderSELF Assessment Inventory

	OK	Want To Focus More	Want To Focus Less

MY SKILLS (List top 3 skills from p 20)
1. _____
2. _____
3. _____

MY FACTUAL KNOWLEDGE (List top 3 areas from p 20)
1. _____
2. _____
3. _____

MY EXPERIENTIAL KNOWLEDGE (List top 3 areas from p 20)
1. _____
2. _____
3. _____

LEADING MY SELF
1. Understanding why I do what I do (insight)
2. Assessing my behavior
3. Accepting help willingly
4. Waiting patiently
5. Making a decision
6. Taking action

7. _____

MY BELIEFS (List top 3 rewritten beliefs from p 34)
1. _____
2. _____
3. _____

MY SELF-TALK (List top 3 or 4 affirmations from p 36)
1. _____
2. _____
3. _____
4. _____

(More on Next Page)

Discovering Your Unique Qualities: LeaderSELF Assessment Inventory

	OK	Want To Focus More	Want To Focus Less

MY GOALS (List top three revised goals from p 41)
1. _____ ____ ____ ____
2. _____ ____ ____ ____
3. _____ ____ ____ ____

LEFT-BRAIN/RIGHT-BRAIN (List your L and R scores from p 46)
1. Total Left-Score: _____ ____ ____ ____
2. Total Right-Score: _____ ____ ____ ____

COMMUNICATION STYLE (List top two items from each category on p 48)

Continue Doing...
1. _____ ____ ____ ____
2. _____ ____ ____ ____

Start Doing...
1. _____ ____ ____ ____
2. _____ ____ ____ ____

Stop Doing...
1. _____ ____ ____ ____
2. _____ ____ ____ ____

COMMUNICATION STYLE PROFILE (Circle your profile from p 63)
1. Director/Ruler ____ ____ ____
2. Thinker/Analyzer ____ ____ ____
3. Relater/Friend ____ ____ ____
4. Socializer/Influencer ____ ____ ____

COMMUNICATION SKILLS
1. Thinking before I speak ____ ____ ____
2. Talking in the group ____ ____ ____
3. Being brief and specific ____ ____ ____
4. Keeping my remarks on the topic ____ ____ ____
5. Being forceful ____ ____ ____
6. Drawing others out ____ ____ ____
7. Listening alertly ____ ____ ____
8. _____ ____ ____ ____

Discovering Your Unique Qualities: LeaderSELF Assessment Inventory

	OK	Want To Focus MORE	Want To Focus LESS

INTERACTING WITH IMPACT-(SOCIAL)
1. Cooperating with others
2. Being helpful
3. Showing empathy
4. Being flexible
5. Standing up for myself
6. Being assertive

7. _____

INTERACTING WITH IMPACT-(MORALE BUILDING)
1. Showing interest
2. Working to keep people from being ignored
3. Harmonizing, helping people reach agreement
4. Reducing tension
5. Standing up for myself
6. Being assertive

7. _____

INTERACTING WITH IMPACT-(OBSERVATION)
1. Noting interest level of the group
2. Noting who talks to whom
3. Noting who is being "left out"
4. Noting when the group avoids a topic
5. Noting tension in the group
6. Separating assumptions about behavior from observations of behavior

7. _____

INTERACTING WITH IMPACT-(TASK FUNCTIONS)
1. Initiator-Information and Opinion Giver
2. Information and Opinion Seeker
3. Initiator and Time Keeper
4. Direction Giver and Recorder
5. Summarizer of Discussion

Discovering Your Unique Qualities: LeaderSELF Assessment Inventory

	OK	Want To Focus More	Want To Focus Less

MANAGING CONFLICT-(FACING EMOTIONAL SITUATIONS)
1. Accepting/Facing my emotions
2. Expressing feelings appropriately
3. Telling others what I feel
4. Disagreeing openly
5. Interpersonal problem solver
6. Accepting tension
7. Being comfortable with silence
8. Facing closeness and affection
9. Facing anger and conflict
10. Facing disappointment
11. Evaluator of emotional conflict
12. _____

GUIDING CHANGE-(PROBLEM SOLVING)
1. Stating problems, issues, and/or goals
2. Asking for opinions
3. Clarifying issues
4. Presenting options
5. Acknowledging full scope of options
6. Evaluating options critically
7. Summarizing the discussion
8. _____

GUIDING CHANGE-(FACILITATION)
1. Coordinator and Liaison
2. Diagnoser of blocks to progress
3. Energizer
4. Reality tester and critic
5. Evaluator of progress to goal attainment
6. Process observer and participant monitor
7. Standard setter and consensus seeker
8. _____

Leading Your Self

Chapter Three

Principle #2: Self-Management (behavioral focus)

> "It's fascinating that as a society we admire the underdog. We root for the underdog. We want the team that came from behind...all season long...to win! Unfortunately, we just don't believe that enough about ourselves... We haven't brought that thinking home to us."   George D'Amico, Former Vice President, MicroWarehouse Inc.

After reading the above perspective, think about this question: "Have you brought the self-confidence, positive-outlook, and winning-spirit home to you?" If so, terrific. If not, don't dismay because within this chapter you will have an opportunity to create your personal vision --of a future yet to be. This process will involve you in reflecting about what's important to you, both personally and professionally. You will also learn about the impact of your beliefs and their influence on your SELF perceptions and the perceptions of others. These ingredients all contribute to heightened self-management.

This chapter also contains information on the practice of engaging in affirmations as a technique for transforming your expectations about life and your future. The segment on motivation underscores that your behavior is basically goal-oriented. And, the goals section will reinforce that clearly defined goals can be extremely motivating, You will also uncover powerful words which either encourage or discourage your motivation to achieve a goal.

> This LeaderSELF guide will provide you with many opportunities for assessing your SELF, learning principles and practices to strengthen your abilities, and apply your enhanced skills to problem-solving opportunities in your life.

Leading Your Self: Creating Purpose and Vision

Creating Your Purpose and Vision Sustains Energy and Passion

If you are similar to other effective people, you want to be part of something significant—something larger than life. You want to do important work and contribute and be appreciated. You want to grow, develop and excel. You want to experience new things. You want to relate to other people whom you trust and respect. And perhaps most of all, you want to make a difference. In short, you want to create meaning and purpose in life.

As you have grown and developed, you have sought to understand the world around you—to figure out what life itself is all about—what it all means. Ultimately, you may have come face to face with the deeper questions about existence itself. Who are you? Why are you here? What skills, abilities and aptitudes do you possess? How can you make a difference, both personally and professionally?

A few people discover or develop a sense of purpose or vision early in their lives. They know who they are and what they want to become at a deep level—and they organize their lives around that purpose. In contrast, most people go through life wishing they had the passion and the energy evidenced by people with a purpose.

The LeaderSELF development program can assist you in discovering a purpose that provides meaning and direction for your life. As you have experienced thusfar, it in-volves a careful examination of your interests, needs, values, and skills—an honest look at yourself—at what energizes you and what drains you of energy. Finally, it entails listening to your innermost intuition, desires, hopes and fears. This self-examination requires a willingness to objectively reassess your self imposed limitations, as well as those real and imagined barriers which may impede your pathway to success.

A compelling personal vision often attracts individuals to its pursuit because it's challenging and it's important. It touches the hunger for meaning that resides in all of us. It energizes and motivates those who choose it at a deep level. It serves as a guide and pathway for decisions and actions in the face of an unknowable future. It also provides the emotional inspiration that keeps people engaged in their pursuits, even when the going gets tough, as it inevitably does in significant undertakings.

Leading Your Self: Creating Purpose and Vision

1. It's a yearning. You'll feel it--it pulls you or attracts you toward one activity over another like a magnet, although it's not tied to glamour or arrogance.

2. It's something that deeply satisfies you. You get a "kick out of doing it". This kind of satisfaction is rarely present when your tasks or strengths are not.

3. The learning is easy. You catch on quickly and it feels exciting to learn.

4. You sense moments of flow. You feel this is something natural for you and you catch glimpses of yourself performing well in this talent area.

> **Your purpose is the internal compass to guide your life and work.**

Creating a Personal Vision

- It is a **Creative Process** of growth and change. Each of us is inherently creative and perpetually engaged in a dynamic process.

- We create ourselves on the basis of how we **Connect** with people, resources, information, circumstances, and events around us.

- **Future Pull** operates as a driving force in each of our lives. We align with this pow-erful process when we develop a compelling vision of the future and commit to achieving it.

Breakpoint and Beyond

Leading Your Self:
Creating Your Purpose and Vision

> **Vision without action is merely a dream.**
> **Action without vision just passes the time.**
> **Vision with action can change the world.**
> **Joel Barker, Futurist**

An effective vision should meet the following requirements:

•**Inspiring**: A vision should give a person a sense of higher purpose, provide meaning and reinforce personal values.

•**Challenging**: A vision has to be challenging, yet realistic. The challenge of the vision should be in tune with the needs of the individual working to attain the vision.

•**Stable, Yet Flexible**: A vision has to remain focused on the most important things. At the same time, it has to be flexible so that it can be adapted to new ways of doing things.

•**Empowering of Self**: A vision should create a mindset that explodes one's narrow range of past-bound possibilities.

•**Providing Direction**: Those who dream of the future choose the future. You can't predict the future, but you can invent it. If you don't know where you are going, then any path will get you there.

> *Being aware of these requirements will enable you to keep focused on what you are doing as you set out to create your vision of the future.*

Leading Your Self: Creating Your Personal Vision

Visioning Activity: The goal of the activity is to assist you in reflecting on and defining your personal vision of a compelling view of a future yet to be.

Part I: Creating Your Life's Focus: Project yourself into the future and imagine that you are looking in retrospect at your life, well-lived. As you review your life you feel a sense of achievement, satisfaction and fulfillment. Identify several words describing key aspects of the experience you have imagined:

_____

_____

Part II: Broadening Your Vision: Answer the following questions as though you have achieved everything in life that you had hoped to accomplish. Use the present tense when answering the questions describing your accomplishments and life.

1. Self-Image: What are your personal qualities and how do you exhibit them in your life? _____

_____

2. Relationships: What types of relationships do you have with family, friends, co-workers, and others? _____

_____

3. Personal Pursuits/Passions: What would you like to create for your life regarding individual learning, service to others, travel, reading, writing, or other activities?

_____

_____

4. Career: What is your ideal profession, vocation, or life's work? What impact do your efforts have? _____

_____

Leading Your Self:
Creating Your Personal Vision

5. Community: What is your vision for the community or society you live in?

_____

_____

6. Health: What is your desire for health, fitness, athletics, nutrition, and anything to do with your body? _____

_____

7. Life Purpose: Imagine that your life has a unique purpose fulfilled through what you do, your interrelationships with others, and the way you live. What is your calling? Describe that purpose. _____

_____

_____

Part III: Clarifying Your Vision: Look at each of the above seven visions you have articulated. Think about what aspects of your visions are closest to your deepest desires and circle the number of your top two choices. Ask yourself these questions as your review your visions:

1. "If I could have it now, would I take it?" This question allows you to dig deeper, clarify what you think, and eliminate those things you truly don't want or value.

2. "Assuming I have it now. What does it bring me?" This question encourages you to reflect on your answers, confirming your values and desires.

For example, someone could have said, "I want to live in Chicago." Then realized, "I want to live in Chicago to be closer to my family." Then, the individual may have revised their vision to read, "I want to have a family and have them be near me."

Colleague Discussion: Like similar individual activities in this LeaderSELF program, the process of creating your purpose and vision can be enhanced by meeting with a colleague and comparing answers to these same questions.

Adopted from P. Senge, The Fifth Discipline Fieldbook.

Leading Your Self: Beliefs

"The mental acceptance of or conviction in the truth or actuality of something."

"Beliefs and assumptions about ourselves and those around us, influence and determine our perceptions of life."

A belief is something we don't know but ACCEPT as TRUE. Our beliefs about ourselves, others and the world are derived from our experiences. Our "belief systems" are the blueprint for our behaviors and emotions. They literally determine the way we perceive life and react to it. Determining what you believe is an important piece of the puzzle for taking control of your life. What you believe is what manifests in your life. If you believe that you deserve happiness, you will find it. If you believe the information and techniques offered within this development program won't work, they won't. If you believe your older brother or sister was right when he called you incompetent as a child, that is what you will be, particularly around him. **If you want to change a belief, you must create a new experience that supports the desired belief.** For example, many people "believed" that the world was flat until Christopher Columbus proved them to be wrong. Many times the beliefs that we had when we were young are changed by the experiences and feedback we receive from others, as we grow older. Sometimes hearing a speech or reading a book or coming to a new understanding as a result of a life experi-ence, can change our beliefs.

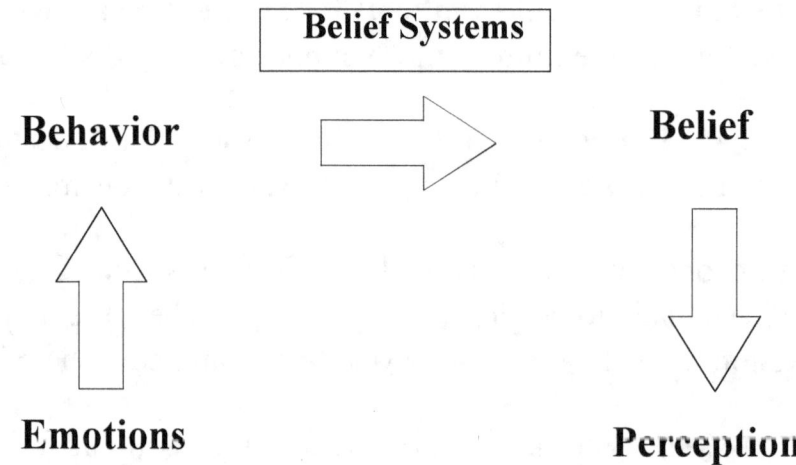

The important aspect to remember about beliefs is that they are changeable! And, the key ingredient that begins the change process is YOU!

Leading Your Self: Beliefs

Following are several techniques to assist you in the process of examining your beliefs. Your responses will provide you with valuable information about yourself. In completing these items, please keep in mind that there are no "right" or "wrong" answers. Also remember that the more honest you are, the more information you will uncover. These exercises are designed to be done quickly. Answer with the first thing that comes to your mind. You may be surprised at the results.

Statement #1: Write 5 sentences beginning with the phrase **"I believe that I..."**
1. _____
2. _____
3. _____
4. _____
5. _____

Statement #2: Write 5 sentences beginning with the phrase **"I believe that in my role as staff member/team member, I..."**
1. _____
2. _____
3. _____
4. _____
5. _____

Statement #3: Write 5 sentences beginning with the phrase **"I believe my team members..."**
1. _____
2. _____
3. _____
4. _____
5. _____

Statement #4: Write 5 sentences beginning with the phrase **"I believe my manager..."**
1. _____
2. _____
3. _____
4. _____
5. _____

Leading Your Self: Beliefs

Part I: When you have completed the sentences on page 33, using the space below, rewrite those sentences to include the beliefs that you would like to have or ones that you feel would be more appropriate.

1. Review your sentences to find any beliefs that are no longer appropriate for who you are today. Rewrite one: _____
_____

2. Review your sentences to find any beliefs that are influenced by others--beliefs that you feel you "should" have. Decide if these beliefs are truly appropriate for who you are today. Rewrite one: _____
_____

3. Review your sentences to find any beliefs that limit your potential or are negative in some way. Rewrite one: _____
_____

4. Refer to the **Criteria for Goal Setting** (page 39). Based on these factors, evaluate each new belief to insure that this belief would be beneficial for you to have.

5. Determine what areas of your life will be affected by these new beliefs. How will your relationships be affected? How will your friends and family react? Consider all the aspects of this new belief and all the aspects of your life that it will influence.

> **Transfer your rewritten beliefs to your LeaderSELF Assessment Inventory on p 22.**

Part II: Once you are satisfied that the new beliefs are appropriate and beneficial, you can integrate them into your belief system.

1. Imagine what you would look like, sound like, and feel like having this belief. What experiences would you have and how would your life be different? Imagine real situa-tions in which having this belief would help you react and feel differently than you did before. Make the images as real as possible and as specific as possible.

2. Practice imagining as often as possible. Repeat the new belief several times, especially when a situation occurs that is related to this belief. The more often you repeat

> **Act as if.....you already have this new belief.**

Leading Your Self: Self-Talk, Creative Visualization and Affirmations

> **Four Basic Steps for Effective Creative Visualization**
> 1. Set your goal.
> 2. Create a clear picture of it.
> 3. Focus on it often.
> 4. Give it positive energy.

Affirmations

To affirm means "to make firm." An affirmation is a strong, positive statement that something is already so. It is a way of "making firm" that which you are imaging.

The practice of engaging in affirmations allows us to begin replacing some of our stale, worn out, or negative mind chatter with more positive ideas and concepts. It is a powerful technique, one which can in a short time transform many of our attitudes and expectations about life, and thereby help to change what we create for ourselves.

Affirmations can be done silently, spoken aloud, written down, or even sung or chanted. Even ten minutes a day of repeating effective affirmations can counterbalance years of old mental habits. An affirmation can be any positive statement. Here are a few just to give you ideas:

Every day in every way I'm getting better and better.
Everything I need is coming to me easily and effortlessly.
I have everything I need to enjoy my here and now.
I am the master of my life.
I love and appreciate myself just as I am.
I am now attracting loving, satisfying relationships into my life.
My relationship with _____ is growing more fulfilling every day.
I always communicate clearly and effectively.
I now have enough time, energy, wisdom, and money to accomplish my dreams.
The more I have, the more I have to give.
I am relaxed and centered. I have plenty of time for everything.
I am enjoying everything I do.
_____ is coming to me, easily and effortlessly.
The light within me is creating miracles in my life here and now.
All things are now working together for good in my life.
I am now attuned to my higher purpose in life.

Leading Your Self: Self-Talk, Creative Visualization and Affirmations

> "When You Want a Change, Change What You Say to Yourself."
> *Shakti Gawain,* <u>Creative Visualization</u>

Things to Remember about Affirmations...

1. Always phrase affirmations in the present tense, not in the future.
2. Always phrase affirmations in the most positive way you can.
3. In general, the shorter and simpler the affirmation, the more effective.
4. Always chose affirmations that feel totally right for you.
5. Always remember that you are creating something new and fresh.
6. Affirmations are not meant to contradict or change your feelings or emotions.
7. Try as much as possible to create a feeling of belief, an experience that your affirmations can be true.

Create Your Own Affirmations: Use the space below to create three or four affirmations. These positive statements should represent what you want most in your life. Consider writing statements that describe your "ideal" experience within your professional and personal life. Refer to p 35 for ideas about your statements and re-member to repeat them to yourself as often as possible.

Affirmation #1: _____
_____

Affirmation #2: _____
_____

Affirmation #3: _____
_____

Affirmation #4: _____
_____

> **Transfer your top three or four affirmations to the Self-Talk section of your LeaderSELF Assessment Inventory on page 22.**

Leading Your Self: Motivation and Behavior

The study of motivation and behavior is a search for answers to perplexing questions about human nature.

Behavior

Behavior is basically goal-oriented. In other words, our behavior is generally motivated by a desire to attain some goal. The goal is not always consciously know by the indi-vidual. All of us wonder many times, "Why did I do that?" A basic unit of behavior is an *activity*. In fact, all behavior is a series of activities. At any given moment we may decide to change from one activity or combination of activities and begin to do something else. This raises some important questions. Why do people engage in one activity and not another? Why do they change activities? How can we managers understand, predict, and even attempt to control what activity or activities a person may engage in at any given moment?

> **To predict behavior, managers must know which motives or needs of people evoke a certain action at a particular time.**

Motives

People differ not only in their ability to do, *but also in their will to do*, or degree of motivation. The motivation of people depends on the strength of their motives. *Motives* are sometimes defined as needs, wants, drives, or impulses within the individual. Mo-tives are directed toward goals, which may be conscious or subconscious. Motives are the "whys" of behavior and the mainsprings of action.

Motivation...

"Incentives that induce people to increase their efforts toward some goal."

Motivating...

"relates to giving Associates/people a reason to do the job and to put forth their best performance."

> **All of our behavior is motivated.**

Leading Your Self: The Motivating Situation

> *Clearly defined goals can be extremely motivating. Goals will keep you on course--keep you doing what's necessary for successful achievement--regardless of whether or not you like the necessary activities.*

Goals

Goals are outside an individual; they are sometimes referred to as "hoped for" rewards toward which motives are directed. *Managers who are successful in motivating Associates are often providing an environment in which appropriate goals are available for need satisfaction.*

    Categories of Activities: <u>Goal-Directed</u> Activity-is motivated behavior directed at reaching a goal.
<u>Goal-Activity-</u>is engaging in the goal itself.

Motivating Situation

The relationship between motives, goals, and activity can be shown as follows:

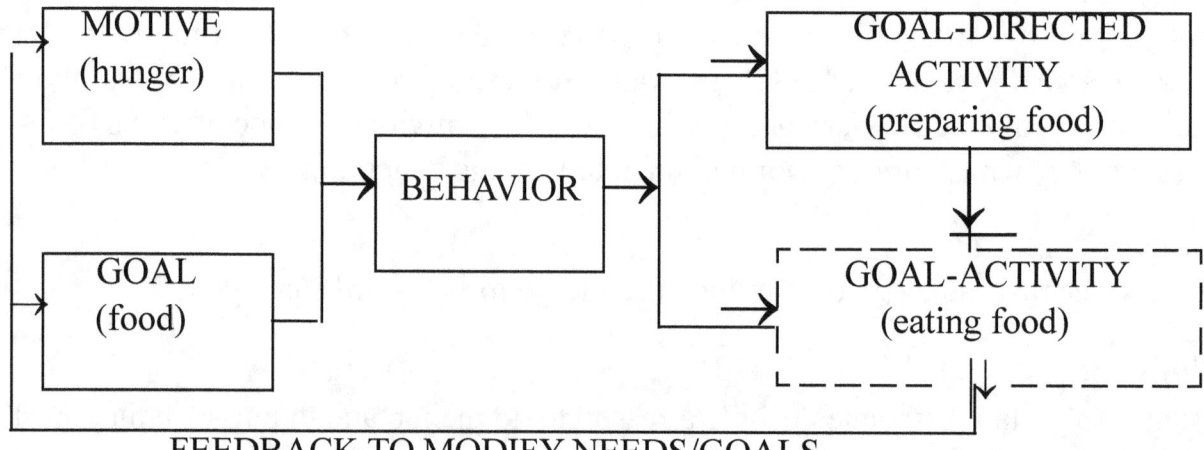

FEEDBACK TO MODIFY NEEDS/GOALS

> **A goal, to be effective, must be appropriate to the need structure of the individual.**

38

Leading Your Self: Criteria for Goal Setting

When asked "what do you want," many people respond "I don't know." Well, if you don't know what you want, how do you know you don't already have it? And, if you don't know what you want, how will you know when you find it? What you want could be available to you and you wouldn't recognize it because you wouldn't know what it is. As a result, you can't possibly get what you want unless you first <u>know</u> what you want.

Goals help you to identify what you want. When it comes to setting goals, be creative. Almost anything is possible if you have a plan to get there. The following **Criteria for Goal Setting** will help you determine goals that are more likely to be beneficial to you.

1. Goals must be within your control.
-You cannot change or control someone else. You can only control your attitude toward them.

2. Goals must be stated using positive statements.
-Eliminate all use of negative language such as "don't," "won't," "can't," etc. Your goal must tell your brain what it is that you want.
-Avoid using the problem as part of the goal (ie: I want to lose weight.)
-Use words that describe the goal in a positive way (ie: I want to develop healthy habits.)

3. Goals must be testable.
-Establish criteria for knowing when you have achieved your goal.

4. Goals must be in your best interest.
-Establish criteria for determining if achieving this goal will be beneficial for you by answering the following questions:
    -How will having this goal affect your life?
    -How is not having this goal beneficial for you?
    -How will your friends and family feel about you having this goal?
    -How important are their reactions to you?
    -What areas of your life will be different?
    -What is stopping you from achieving this goal?
    -What will you be giving up in order to achieve this?
    -What are you willing to do to achieve this goal?
    -What other questions would be appropriate to ask in relation to this goal?

Leading Your Self: Goals and Action Planning

> **The first two letters of the word "GOAL" are "GO."**

Individual Activity: Use the space below to write down two or three goals that you would like to accomplish. **Refer to your top three priorities identified on p. 17.**

Goal #1: _____
_____

Goal #2: _____
_____

Goal #3: _____
_____

Seven Modal Operators

After you have written down your goals, think about each of the following words, and consider SUBSTITUTING one of these for one of your existing words in your goal statement... *if* you think the word appears to be "stronger" or more positive.

#1: "I SHOULD"...What is your reaction to this word? "Shoulds" in life are often "what OTHER people want us to do. (ie: "You really SHOULD call your mother more often.")

#2: "I MUST"...What kind of reaction do you have to this word? "Musts" in life are often extremely POLARIZING. The response to a MUST is often, "You and what army are going to make me do it?

#3: "I WILL"...What about this word? "Wills" in life, (not the written ones) are often extremely MOTIVATING. When someone repeats, the two words, "I WILL" vocally and mentally, they are establishing an intention focused on attaining a goal.

#4: "I WANT"...What kind of reaction do you have to this word? Is it a strong reaction? Does it sound like your goal is possible? "Wants" in life often describe one's desires. The response to a WANT is often, "I will do whatever it takes to obtain this goal.

Leading Your Self: Goals and Action Planning

#5: "I CAN"...What about your reaction to this word? Keep in mind that your tone of voice in saying the word CAN, will determine the effectiveness of this word within a goal statement. If someone uses the word CAN as a type of question. It can be interpreted as someone needing "permission" from someone else to strive for it. However, if the word CAN is used with a sense of conviction that I have the ability, knowledge, and experience to strive for a particular goal, then the word can greatly influence one's prob-ability of goal attainment.

#6: "I AM",,,What is your reaction to this word? When you phrase a goal as already being experienced, you strengthen the probability of it's attainment. This approach acts as an affirmation; a strong, positive statement that something is already so.

#7: "I MAY"...Finally, what type of reaction do you have to this word? "Mays" in life, imply that one has to ask permission from someone BEFORE the goal may be considered. It is a tentative word that doesn't contribute to accomplishment of one's goals.

Summary: These seven words are "modal operators," or "trigger" words influencing our minds interpretation of whether or not something is attainable. These words are strong, **INDEPENDENT** of the goal itself. Some people combine modal operator words such as, "I want, I can, I will..." creating an especially powerfully combination for goal attainment. Consider rewriting one or more of your goals from the previous page, using modal operator words that are meaningful to you. **Transfer your revised goals to your LeaderSELF Assessment Inventory on page 23.**

Revised Goal #1: _____

Revised Goal #2: _____

Revised Goal #3: _____

When you use the modal operator word or words that inspire you to strive for a goal, you are more likely to attain it.

Leading Your Self: Goals and Action Planning

An **Action Plan** is an outline of who will do what, when and by what methods, when you are ready to implement a solution. It ensures that nothing is left to chance as you set out to implement a new way of doing things.

Steps to Create an Action Plan
1. Brainstorm what needs to be done.
2. On a chart, decide what needs to be done.
3. Decide who will do what.
4. Determine how it will be done.
5. Identify what resources will be needed.
6. Determine if there are any special circumstances or needs to be taken into account.

Key Elements of an Action Plan Worksheet

GOAL: _____

Date to Be Completed	Action to Be Taken	Methods	People Involved	Resources Needed	Special Needs
Date Needed	Brainstorm what needs to be done	How will your goal be done?	Who is involved?	Time? Money? Motivation?	Advice

---

The Action Plan "Rule of Three"

Rule #1: Create Your Goals
Rule #2: Identify Your Obstacles
Rule #3: Determine Your Countermeasures to Overcome the Obstacles

"Never give in--never, never, never, in nothing great or small..." Winston

Leading Your Self: Action Planning Worksheet

NAME: _____

GOAL: _____

Date to Be Completed	Action to Be Taken	Methods	People Involved	Resources Needed	Special Needs

Interacting with Others

Chapter Four

Principle #3: Interacting with Others (interpersonal focus)

"To be or not to be, that is the question" is one of the most famous soliloquies in literature. Within Act III, Scene One, Shakespeare describes Hamlet as struggling with the difficulty of acting under the weight of a thought "which makes cowards of us all." Hamlet, on the edge of despair, asks himself why he, when he has so many reasons, cannot stir himself to action… Now, we don't claim to be Shakespearean scholars. But, we believe that Hamlet is attempting to reconcile his struggle between *what he knows and what he feels…*

A parallel in 21st Century life finds each one of us attempting to reconcile what we know, our intellect, with what we feel, our emotions. We all know that IQ or Intelligence Quotient measures an individual's raw reasoning ability. Studies have demonstrated that IQ measures alone cannot predict success in life. Best selling author Daniel Goleman in his book, Emotional Intelligence suggests that at best, IQ contributes about 20% to the factors that determine life success, which leaves 80% to other forces.

Certainly, many of the LeaderSELF principles comprise the 80% of "other forces" contributing to your success. Of particular importance are your skills associated with interpersonal communication, interaction, and relationships. In fact, your undertaking to strengthen your ability to interact with others is a lifelong endeavor.

With the idea of continuous improvement in mind, each one of us can benefit from further understanding and strengthening of our interpersonal skills. This chapter will provide opportunities for you to enhance your skills and abilities through learning about your own and others thinking and communicating styles and preferences. You will learn that one's "strengths" can sometimes turn into "weaknesses," when the individual is under stress. You will also discover strategies for interacting with impact with many different types of people.

Are You Left-Brained or Right-Brained? (An Assessment)

The questionnaire below is designed to provide you with a "profile" which identifies the strength of your left-brain and right-brain characteristics (see pg 43 for description of characteristics).

Directions: Circle the number that best describes how you operate in a particular situ-ation. An L5 indicates the strongest inclination for the tendency described; an R5 shows a strong opposite tendency. **You may circle a number in both columns.** Go with your first impulse and consider your behavior both at work and at home--where you prob-ably have more freedom to plan your day as you wish.

Do you start each day by making a list, set-ting priorities and sticking to them?	Or do you like to jump in and plan as you go?

L5..........4............3...........2............1...........0..........1..........2..........3............4............R5

Do you stick to the same routine every morning?	Or do you alter your routine based on the way you feel and find yourself to be fairly unpredictable?

L5..........4............3...........2............1...........0..........1..........2..........3............4............R5

Do you prefer to finish one thing before starting another?	Or do you enjoy moving back and forth between projects?

L5..........4............3...........2............1...........0..........1..........2..........3............4............R5

Is it important to maintain routine systems of organizaton, and does it bother you when others disregard your system?	Or do you frequently change your rou-tines and find it boring to always do things the same way?

L5..........4............3...........2............1...........0..........1..........2..........3............4............R5

Do you get irritated by changes in your schedule or when a friend pops over un-announced?	Or can you easily shift gears and enjoy the surprise?

L5..........4............3...........2............1...........0..........1..........2..........3............4............R5

Do you prefer several days notice before going out of town or having guests over for dinner?	Or are you always ready for spur-of-the moment opportunities?

L5..........4............3...........2............1...........0..........1..........2..........3............4............R5

Are You Left-Brained or Right-Brained?
(An Assessment)

When asked to help on a project, do you check previous commitments, saying "no" when you are too busy?	Or do you say "yes," only to realize later that you are spread too thin?

L5..........4............3............2............1...........0..........1...........2............3.............4............R5

Do you enjoy following through with details on projects?	Or would you rather come up with a new idea, promote it, then let someone else handle all the details?

L5..........4............3............2............1...........0..........1...........2............3.............4............R5

If you have a big project to complete, do you barricade yourself in a room with no distractions and work until it is completed?	Or do you spread everything out on the table or floor, turn on some music, make a pleased?

L5..........4............3............2............1...........0..........1...........2............3.............4............R5

At the end of the day, do you clean up your work area at home or at the office because you don't like to come back to clutter?	Or do you leave unfinished work out on the desk so you can pick up where you left off?

L5..........4............3............2............1...........0..........1...........2............3.............4............R5

Total L Score:_____   Total R Score:_____

ASSESSMENT SCORING

Add up the numbers circled in each column and put the total in the space above for both total "L" scores and total "R" scores. The left column describes typical traits of a left-brain-oriented person, while the right column depicts right-brain traits. The column you scored higher in should generally indicate the extent of your dominance. But before you analyze your score, note that many people behave in a left-brain manner at work but in a right-brain manner at home. Thus, your answers pertaining to how you behave at home may carry more weight than those regarding how you behave at the office.

A score of 40 or more on either side usually indicates a strong dominance, especially if the total of the other column is less than 20. If both scores fall within 15 points of each other, you have an integrated working style. This has many advantages. First, it allows you to be flexible rather than rigid as you go about your day. But also, whole-brain people get the best of both worlds by adding structure to their creative and spontaneous activities and by adding creative insights to logic-oriented problem-solving tasks. (For more info see: <u>Building Brain Power by</u> Ann McGee-Cooper)

Left-Brain and Right-Brain Characteristics

Right Hemisphere

- Irrational
- Illogical
- Holistic
- Spontaneous
- Feelings
- Imagination
- Art, Music, Dance
- Mime, Theatre
- Intuition
- Spatial
- People-Oriented
- "Let's Do It"
- Creative
- Think in Pictures
- Dreamer
- Playful
- 3-D Thinking

Left Hemisphere

- Rational
- Logical
- Linear
- Sequential
- Facts
- Knowledge
- Language, Math, Law
- Systems
- Rules
- Symbols
- Fact-Oriented
- "Let's Plan First!"
- Implement
- Think in Words and Figures
- Worker
- Serious
- 2-D Thinking

"The more connections that can be made in the brain, the more integrated the experience is within memory."
        Don Campbell

"If the brain is a computer, then it is the only one that runs on glucose, generates 10 watts of electricity, and is manufactured by unskilled labor."
        David Lewis

Communication...A Definition

> "Communication is the use of words and
> other symbols to achieve various outcomes"
>
> "Communication, the exchange of information and
> opinions, is the key to all relationships"

Personal Communication Styles

A. List three of your best communication qualities.
   (These are things you want to **continue doing**.)

   1. _____
   2. _____
   3. _____

B. List three communication qualities that you don't have but would like to have.
   (These are things you want to **start doing**.)

   1. _____
   2. _____
   3. _____

C. List three of your behaviors that block effective communication.
   (These are things you want to **stop doing**.)

   1. _____
   2. _____
   3. _____

> **Transfer two of your communication qualities from each category to the LeaderSELF Assessment Inventory (LAI) on p 23**

> *Through Effective Communication, the sender and the receiver both share responsibility for mutual understanding*

Linear Communication: One Way

SENDER

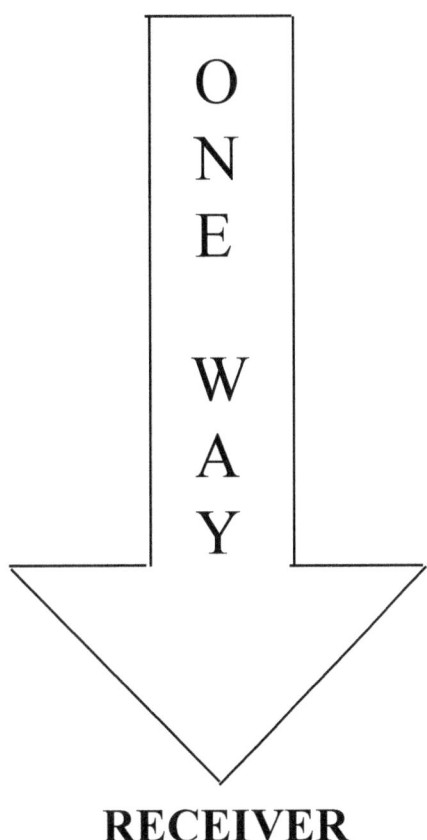

RECEIVER

Linear or one way communication involves only one speaker and one or more listeners. The speaker is usually giving commands or directions. This type of communication is effective in situations which require no discussion, no feedback.

List some examples of how linear communication is used in the work place:
1. _____
2. _____
3. _____

Advantages: Disadvantages:
1. _____   1. _____
2. _____   2. _____
3. _____   3. _____
4. _____   4. _____

Communicating to Understand: Two Way/Interactive

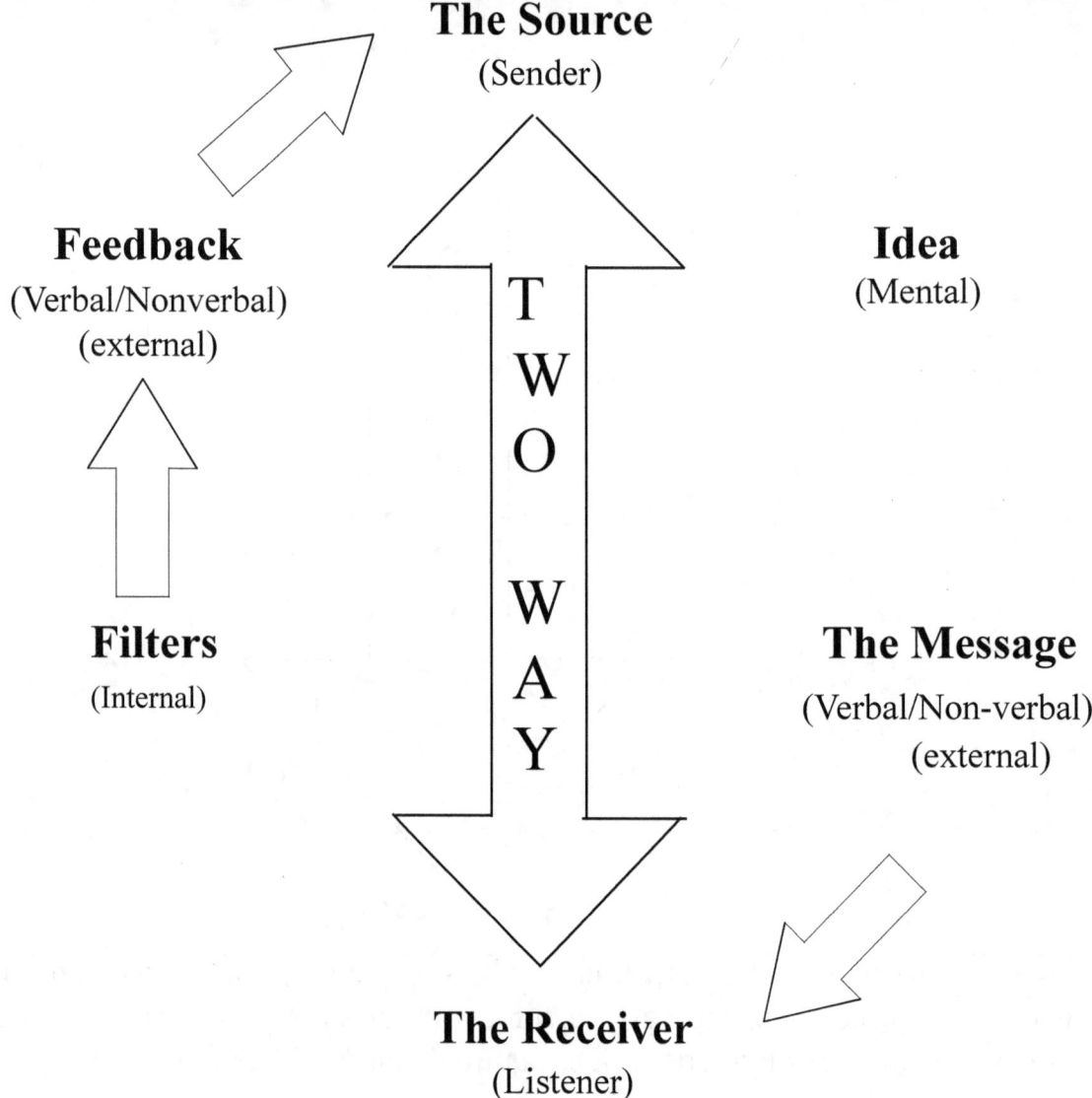

*In this model, communication is viewed as dynamic and interactive-The path of communication is circular as each element is set in motion and the process ends where it started.

*The external, visible, observable actions are focused on the interaction between the **SENDER** (source) and the **RECEIVER** (listener). However, the source or sender begins the exchange as a result of an internal process of an **IDEA** (thought, information) which is encoded in the form of a **MESSAGE** (words, gestures, tone of voice, and perhaps visual aids).

Two Way Communication (continued)

*The **MESSAGE** travels through a medium or means of communication to the **RECEIVER** (listener).

*The next step in the communication process is when the Recipient of this message internally processes the message by making meaning from the information and extracting value from ideas.

***FILTERS**, internal to each individual, are important at this stage because they can both assist or impede communication. Because filters "screen" how we perceive a message, they can unconsciously reinforce our existing thoughts/views which may prevent us from viewing people, an event, or concept more objectively.

Examples of filters include:
- Emotional Feelings   -Age   -Economic Status   -Cultural Background
- Gender   -Language   -Education   -Life Experiences

***FEEDBACK**, both verbal and non-verbal, is the receivers external, visible observable actions which are designed to demonstrate the listener's ability to hear, understand, evaluate, and respond to the sender's idea. This phase generally allows the listener to become the speaker and the cycle continues.

The Two-Way Communication Process

One important element is that the Receiver has to be "ready to hear the message." The other important element is that there is "EXTERNAL NOISE" which might be going on while two people are talking, distracting one or both of them from their conversa-tion. There is also "INTERNAL NOISE," or internal FILTERS that may screen out information being heard. Examples: **Internal Noise:** daydreaming, thinking about last night's _____, anticipating today's _____, planning for tomorrow's _____ or general stress in a person's life that distracts them from the conversation at hand. **Internal Filters:** emotional feelings, economic status, gender, education level, job status, individual differences, age, cultural background, language or life experiences.

CAUTION: Filters help us to screen out and categorize information which can be helpful to us, and actually **assist** us in communicating. However, they can also serve as defenses, pre-conceived ideas and perceptions which can **impede** our ability to communicate. So it is extremely important to be aware of our filters.

Interactive or Interpersonal Communication: Two Way

Interpersonal communication can be defined as communication involving two or more people in which each takes turns being the speaker and the listener. The listener understands the **meaning** of what the speaker said. **Both** the listener and the speaker have to work together effectively to make sure this happens.

List some examples of how interactive communication is used in the work place?

1. _____
2. _____
3. _____

Advantages of interactive communication:

1. _____
2. _____
3. _____

Disadvantages of interactive communication:

1. _____
2. _____
3. _____

Effective communication depends upon two people working together.

Many people approach communication as though it were the simple process of one person telling something to another.

Interpersonal Communication

"The ability to express an idea is as important as the idea itself"
Bernard Baruch

According to professor Albert Mehrabian of UCLA, one of the foremost experts in personal communications, there are three elements that comprise communication: the **verbal** which is the message itself, the words you say; the **vocal** which is the intonation, projection and resonance of the voice that carries those words; and the **visual** element which is what people see of your face and your body.

The key ingredient to effective communicating is BELIEVABILITY!

Behavioral Skills: The Key Elements of Interpersonal Communication.

> **Eye Communication-** Keep your listeners involved and engaged by maintaining 3-6 second contact with as many as possible.
>
> **Posture/Movement-** Change the dynamics of your presentation with purposeful movement. Whenever possible, move around but never backup from your listener.
>
> **Gesture/Facial Movement-** Smile, a "real" smile and be careful for nervous gestures.
>
> **Voice/Vocal Variety -** Your voice transmits energy. Your vocal tone and quality can count for much of "Your Message." Use vocal variety and stay clear of a monotone. Emphasize the right word.
>
> **Articulation-**The following areas all deal with improving speech.
> •Posture   •Voice Obstacles   •Slang   •Technical Jargon   •Non-Words
>
> **Listener Involvement -** ...To maintain the active interest and involvement of each person with whom you are communicating, every time you talk--whether one person or one thousand.
>
> **Humor-** Begin with a friendly, warm comment and make your humor appropriate.
>
> **The Natural Self-** Be yourself in all communication circumstances.
>
> **Dress/Appearance -** The most important two words for effective dress are **"be appropriate."**

Barriers to Effective Communication

> ****MESSAGE BREAKDOWN****
>
> Our **Verbal Message** equals **10% of our message** (words)
>
> Our **Non-Verbal** message equals **90% of our message**
> (body language, tone, pitch, eye contact, gestures)

Perception - A combination of three elements: our past experiences, how we view the present communication situation, and our motivations in the present situation. Interpretations exist because of perceptions.

Unspoken Expectations - Assumptions based on past experience.

Prejudgments - When we come to a decision without fully understanding the facts.

Self-Fulfilling Prophecies - When you "tell" yourself what the outcome of a situation will be before it happens.

Language - What we say, the words we use:
   Vagueness - Being too brief, not offering enough pertinent information.
   Verbosity - Talking too much, giving too much detail.
   Jargon - The special vocabulary of a particular group or activity.
   Slang - Common phrases in a social setting that have no place in the workplace
   Profanity - Unacceptable in any working arena.

> **CAUTION: COMMUNICATION IN PROGRESS**
>
> **People hear only 25% of what we say:**
> We <u>hear</u> at a rate of 150 words per minute
> We <u>listen</u> at a rate of 300 words per minute
>
> Our brain <u>processes</u> at a rate of 600 words per minute

Pacing and Leading: Dynamics of Persuasion

Effective communication is the result of the skillful integration of many factors, most occurring so naturally that we are usually unaware of them. Two of the key elements of communication are:

Pacing

Pacing is essentially matching another person's "rhythm": their body posture, their breathing, their tone-of-voice, their rate-of-speech, etc. By asking various questions and observing their reactions, you become aware of certain aspects of the person's behavior and then "match" them by adopting their behavior. This establishes an **unconscious rapport between you.**

Although pacing occurs automatically in most interactions, if you are not effectively communicating with someone, *you might find you are mismatched in some way.* Try pacing them to improve the rapport, and then lead them to an understanding of your point-of-view.

Leading

When you lead someone, you must have a definite purpose for the discussion in mind. This is the "persuasion" part of communication. In order to convince someone of the merit of your idea or opinion, you must "lead" them to a specific conclusion, taking them one step at a time until they reach the destination. There are various techniques for doing this, and some of them are listed below:

1. **Skillful questioning** directs the person's thinking by skillfully asking questions of another....helping to direct them to the same conclusion as yourself.
2. **Anchoring** is effective if used at an appropriate time during a discussion to connect their idea to one of your own.
3. **Overlapping** leads to new ways of thinking when you "agree" with the first half of their statement and then finish the sentence with your own statement.
4. **Future pacing** enables you to create a new image by providing an individual with the opportunity to anticipate the future...(ie: You have had this experience. "Now think about **the next time** (future)....how would you respond?)
5. The **tone of your voice** and your rate of speech can affect the client's mood, making them excited or calming them down.

Predicate Phrases/Words

Predicates in Neuro Linguistic Programming (NLP) are the descriptive words and phrases people use to communicate their perceptions of the world. Most commonly, they are represented visually, auditorily, or kinesthetically. Effective communication is easily achieved by matching the predicates used by the listener. In this way, the listener can readily understand the meaning of the communication.

> Do You **See** What I Mean?

VISUAL (see) Phrases

an eyeful	in person	see to it
appears to me	in view of	short-sighted
bird's eye view	looks like	showing off
catch a glimpse of	make a scene	sight for sore eyes
clear-cut	mental image	staring into space
dim view	mind's eye	take a peek eye to
eye	naked eye	tunnel vision
paint a picture	get a perspective on	up front
plainly see	well-defined	hazy idea
point-of-view	in light of	pretty as a picture

VISUAL(see) Words

analyze	anger	appear
bright	clarity	clear
cognizant	conspicuous	demonstrate
dream	examine	focus
foresee	hindsight	idea
illusion	illustrate	imagine
inspect	look	notice
obscure	observe	obvious
perception	perspective	picture
pinpoint	reflect	scene
scope	scrutinize	show
sketchy	survey	vague
view	vista	watch

Predicate Phrases/Words

Do You **Hear** What I Am Saying?

AUDITORY (hear) Phrases

after-thought	blabber-mouth	clear as a bell
clearly expressed	call on	describe in detail
earful	express yourself	give an account of
give me your ear	grant an audience	hear me out hid-
den message	inquire into	in tune key-note
speaker	listen to this	loud and clear
manner of speaking	pay attention to	power of speech
out-spoken	rap session	rings a bell state
your purpose	tattletale	to tell the truth
tongue-tied	tuned in/tuned out	unheard of utterly
voiced an opinion	well-informed	within hearing range
word for word		

AUDITORY (hear) Words

announce	articulate	call
clicks	communicate	converse
dictate	discuss	divulge
earshot	enunciate	gossip
hear	hush	inquire
interview	listen	loud
mention	noise	oral
proclaim	pronounce	remark
report	resonant	ring roar
rumor	said say	scream
screech shrill	silence	sound
speak	speechless	squeal
state	talk	tell tone
utter	vocal voice	whisper
yell		

Predicate Phrases/Words

> Can You Get in **Touch** With this?

KINESTHETIC (Feel) Phrases

all washed up	boils down to	chip off the old block
come to grips with	control yourself	cool/calm/collected
firm foundation	floating on air	get a handle on get a
load of this	get in touch with	get the drift of get
your goat	hand-in-hand	hang in there heated
argument	hold it	hold on hot-head
keep in touch	keep your shirt on	know-how
lay cards on the table	light-headed	moment of panic
not following you	pull some strings	sharp as a tack
slipped my mind	smooth operator	so-so
start from scratch	stiff upper lip stuffed shirt	underhanded

KINESTHETIC (Feel) Words

active	affected	bearable
callous	charge	concrete
dull	emotional feel	firm
foundation	grasp	grip
handle	hanging	hassle
heated	hold	hustle
intuition	lukewarm	moves
motion	muddles	munch
numb	panicky	pressure
punch	rough	rush
sense	sensitive	shallow
shift	slam smooth	soft
solid	sore	stress
structure	support	tension
tied	touch	unbearable
unsettled	warm	whipped

Visual, Auditory and Kinesthetic Cues

Verbal cues which reveal an individual's perceptions - Experts in the field of neurolinguistics have concluded that people express themselves in terms of how they perceive the world--and according to which senses affect them most strongly. Before you can understand how you can adapt your listening style to communicate better, you need to examine some typical examples which fall within the following three categories: Visual, Auditory and Kinesthetic.

Visual: Individuals with a strong visual orientation might respond to your suggestion by saying:
"I see your point."   "I can envision that."
"That looks good to me."   "I can't get clear on what you mean."
"I think your reasonings fuzzy."   "I don't understand your focus."

Auditory: Individuals who favor a strong auditory orientation might respond in the following ways:
"I hear you."   "What I hear doesn't impress me."
"It comes through loud and clear." "I'm not tuned into this idea."
"Sounds good/Doesn't sound good to me." "It's too complicated."

Kinesthetic: Iindividuals who favor a strong kinesthetic orientation rely on "gut feelings," sensation and sensory learning and might say things like:
"I feel good about that."   "That feels right."
"I have a gut feeling about that." "I don't feel like that the right approach."

Put a check mark in front of the description that best describes you within 1A-1C, 2A-2C, 3A-3C, and 4A-4C. (Note about statements: A's are Visual, B's are Auditory and C's are Kinesthetic.)

___1A. Puts equipment together using printed directions.

___1B. Has someone else read directions when putting together equipment.

___1C. Puts equipment together using sense of touch.

___2A. Frequently makes, uses, and relies on daily "lists."

___2B. Plans daily schedule by "talking it through" with someone else.

___2C. No schedule. Prefers action to structure.

___3A. Communicates best by writing.

___3B. Communicates best by talking.

___3C. Gestures are a critical part of communication style.

___4A. Reads/writes in spare time.

___4B. Listens to music in spare time.

___4C. Uses spare time for physical activities and keeping fit.

Personal Style Exercise

The Personal Style Survey is a selected list of statements that describes visible and observable actions of people in relation to their preferences for Directness, Indirectness, People, and Task.

By completing a Personal Style survey, you will be able to determine your Style & The Style of others.

	Indirect	Direct
Task	Analyzer	Director
People	Relater	Socializer

"People have one thing in common;
We are all different."

Pick a Personal Style, Any Style

People have one thing in common: they are all different"

Robert Zend

Check one word from each pair, responding to the statement, "If I were forced to choose, I would say...I am..." Think of your role within the company and pick the one that applies 51% of the time or more. Answer all.

Description	A	Description	B
Approaches risk, decisions or change quickly	_____	Approaches risk, decisions or change slowly	_____
Frequent contributor to group conversations	_____	Infrequent contributor to group conversations	_____
Frequent use of gestures to emphasize points	_____	Infrequent use of gestures to emphasize points	_____
Often makes statements: "I'm positive"	_____	Often makes qualified statements "I think so"	_____
Emphasizes points thru confident vocal statements	_____	Emphasizes points thru explanation of information	_____
Questions tend to emphasize points	_____	Questions tend to be for clarification or support	_____
Less Patient; competitive	_____	More patient and cooperative	_____
Confronting, controlling	_____	Diplomatic; collaborative	_____
Intense; assertive	_____	Understated; reserved	_____
Tends to bend or break established rules	_____	Tends to follow established rules	_____
More challenging	_____	More accepting	_____
More talkative	_____	More quiet	_____

Total_____

Total the check marks in Column A and put the score on the Total line.
Then circle the Total number on the horizontal line on the graph.

Pick a Personal Style, Any Style

Description	C	Description	D
Shows & Shares feelings freely	_____	Keeps feelings private	_____
Makes most decisions based on feelings (subjective)	_____	Makes most decisions based on facts (objective)	_____
Conversation includes digressions	_____	Focuses conversation on issues /tasks	_____
More relaxed and warm	_____	More formal and proper	_____
Goes with the flow	_____	Goes with the agenda	_____
Opinion oriented	_____	Fact-oriented	_____
Easy to get to know in business situations	_____	Takes time to get to know in business situations	_____
Flexible about how their time is used by others	_____	Disciplined about how their time is used by others	_____
Prefers to work with others	_____	Prefers to work independently	_____
Shows more enthusiasm than most	_____	Shows less enthusiasm than most	_____
Responsive to dreams, visions & concepts	_____	Responsive to realities, actual experiences & facts	_____
More people-oriented	_____	More task-oriented	_____

Total _____

Total the check marks in column D and put that score on the Total line. Then circle the Total number on the vertical line in the

Pick a Personal Style, Any Style

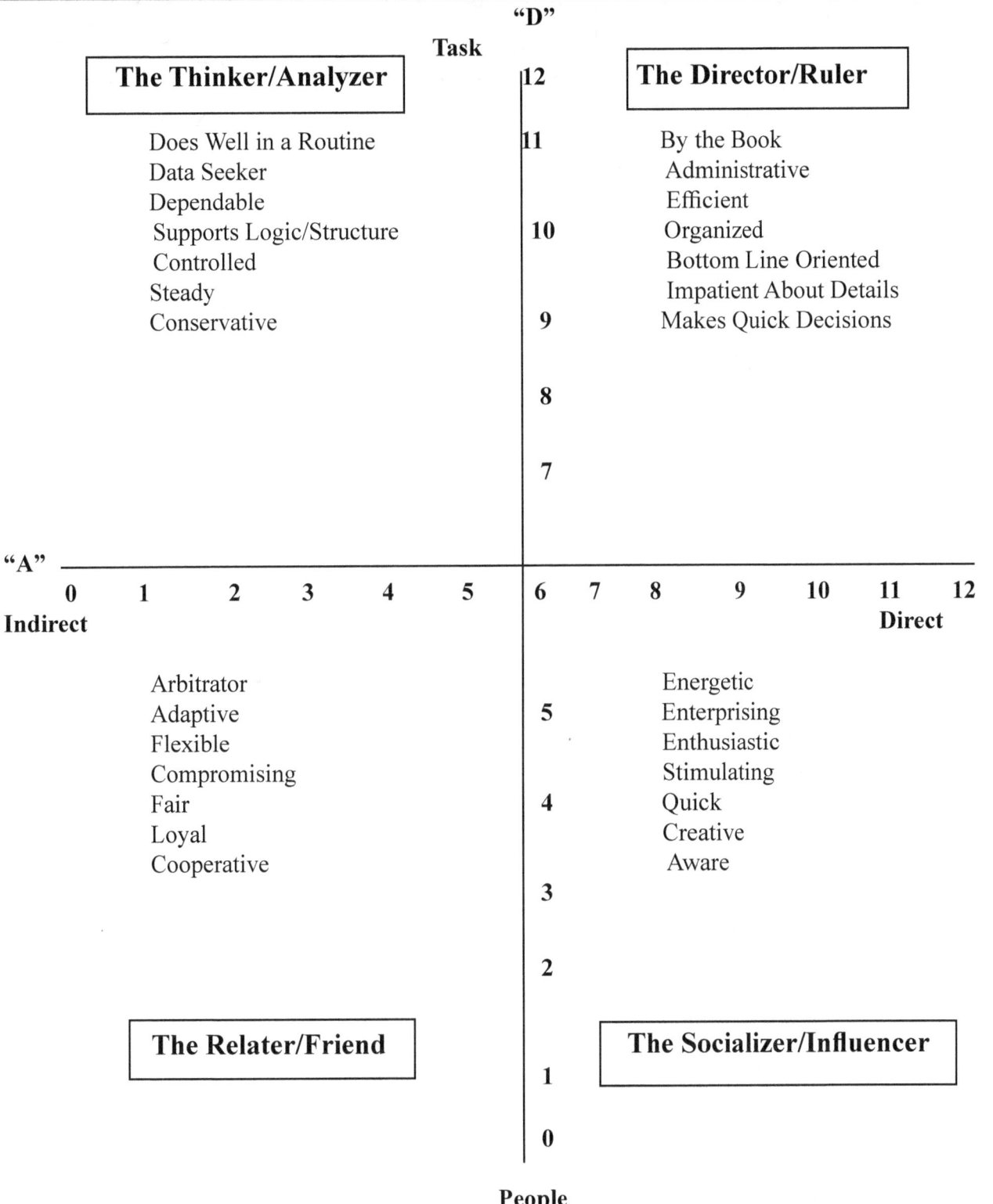

Summary Of Behavioral Styles

	RELATER	**THINKER**	**DIRECTOR**	**SOCIALIZER**
BEHAVIOR PATTERN	Open/Indirect	Self-Contained/Indirect	Self-Contained/Direct	Open/Direct
APPEARANCE	• Casual • Conforming	• Formal • Conservative	• Businesslike • Functional	• Fashionable • Stylish
WORK-SPACE	• Personal • Relaxed • Friendly • Informal	• Structured • Organized • Functional • Formal	• Busy • Formal • Efficient • Structured	• Stimulating • Personal • Cluttered • Friendly
PACE	Slow/Easy	Slow/Systematic	Fast/Decisive	Fast/Spontaneous
PRIORITY	Maintaining relationships	The task: the process	The task: the results	Relationships Interacting
FEARS	Confrontation	Embarrassment	Loss of control	Loss of prestige
UNDER TENSION WILL	Submit/Acquiesce	Withdraw/Avoid	Dictate/Assert	Attack/Be sarcastic
SEEKS	Attention	Accuracy	Productivity	Recognition
NEEDS TO KNOW (BENEFITS)	• How it will affect his or her personal circumstances	• How to justify the purchase logically • How it works	• What it does • By when • What it costs	• How it enhances his or her status • Who else uses it
GAINS SECURITY BY	Close relationships	Preparation	Control	Flexibility
WANTS TO MAINTAIN	Relationships	Credibility	Success	Status
SUPPORT HIS OR HER	Feelings	Thoughts	Goals	Ideas
ACHIEVES ACCEPTANCE BY	• Conformity • Loyalty	• Correctness • Thoroughness	• Leadership • Competition	• Playfulness • Being Entertaining
LIKES YOU TO BE	Pleasant	Precise	To the point	Stimulating
WANTS TO BE	Liked	Correct	In Charge	Admired
IRRITATED BY	• Insensitivity • Impatience	• Surprises • Unpredictability	• Inefficiency • Indecision	• Inflexibility • Routine
MEASURES PERSONAL WORTH BY	• Compatibility with others • Depth of relationships	• Precision • Accuracy • Activity	• Results • Track record • Measurable progress	• Acknowledgment • Recognition • Applause • Compliments
DECISIONS ARE	Considered	Deliberate	Definite	Spontaneous

Behavioral Flexibility

The underlying needs for each of the four personality types are quite basic:
The <u>Director's</u> need is to get the job done. The Socializer wants to be noticed. The Thinker is concerned about accuracy. The <u>Relater</u> wants to maintain good relationships.

CAUTION: Every personality includes Relater, Thinker, Socializer, and Director traits. In order to relate to those underlying needs, you need to develop **behavioral flexibility**-t*he ability to adapt your own behavior appropriately to meet the needs of the person your are dealing with.*

If you hear <u>Director</u> behavior in a person, the first thing you want to do is to get to the point and then show them what the options are. Put the decision in the Director's hands.

When you are communicating with a <u>Thinker,</u> be prepared to walk through each step. Focus on accuracy and don't rush into your conclusion. The Thinker wants to fully understand each detail along the way. Stick to your agenda, be logical, precise, and accurate.

In dealing with a <u>Relater</u>, they are very easy going. However, they are cautious about making quick decisions. Focus on developing a relationship. This personality type needs to feel comfortable with you before anything can happen. The Relater needs to be able to trust you. Take your time, put him or her at ease, and answer all questions fully.

The Bottom Line: **Learn to treat people the way they want to be treated**.

When you **modify your behavior** and allow that person to remain in his or her own comfort zone, tension will be reduced.

When tension goes down, cooperation goes up. When cooperation goes up...
so does your **IMPACT!!**

Behavioral Styles

The choices we make in life give people clues about our personality.

What about the type of job Directors seek? A Director is strong, forceful, outgoing, competitive, and needs to be in control. They choose jobs that let them be in control. Managers, physicians, sales managers, drill sergeants; no matter what they are doing, they will run the job like a command post.

What type of job would the Thinker seek? Anything that has to do with the technical aspect of a particular field. Research, accounting, computers, and science. Thinkers are the technicians of the world.

What type of job is the Relater drawn toward? The helping professions- personnel, education, medicine, counseling, psychology, human resource development, and religious vocations.

What type of job is the Socializer drawn to? They choose public relations, performing arts, selling, advertising, and professional speaking. In other words, anything that puts them in the spotlight. They need to be where the action is.

Caution: Every personality includes Director, Thinker, Relater and Socializer traits. The behavior you see at any given time, tells you what the person's needs are at that moment.

In summary, when you interact with someone, he or she will relate to you in a very predictable pattern consistent with their personality type. The more you can tune in to an individual's way of thinking and making choices, the more likely you will be able to build rapport and strengthen your relationship with them.

Interpreting the Four Styles When Interacting With Others

> **People will teach you how to interact with them ...**
> **If you will pay attention to the messages they send you.**

Management and control of the tension level is one of the most effective things a person can do to increase the likelihood of positive impact. Remember, when tension is up, trust and cooperation are down. But when tension is down, trust and cooperation rise.

An extremely effective way of reducing tension is to adjust your way of communicating to accommodate the other person's way of communicating. To do this, you learn to "read" other people and communicate to them in a way that maintains their comfort zone. In fact, people will teach you how to treat them if you pay attention to their verbal, vocal, and body communication.

Impact Strategies are based on building long-term relationships with others. With this in mind, we need to know how to make relationships work for us. This focus on relation-ships increases our awareness of how to deal with different people in different ways. When you attempt to influence others, you want to know what you can do to put them at ease, reduce the tension level, and open communication so that you can communicate your ideas and be of assistance to them. That's IMPACT!

Direct & Indirect Behavior

One way to recognize the best strategy is by observing the level of directness in a person's behavior. There is a marked difference between direct and indirect behavior. On a scale from direct to indirect, very **direct** people seek to control circumstances, information, or other people by taking charge. They step right in and initiate action. **Indirect** people prefer a slower, easier going pace. They are often a little more tactful and will consider their actions carefully.

Direct people tend to be rather blunt and to the point. Indirect people ask you if you'd "like" to do something rather than tell you "what" to do. Direct people are often risk takers because they like to get on with their lives and their business. They like forward motion. Indirect people prefer to avoid risk, so they will take the least risky way of approaching a situation.

Interpreting the Four Styles When Interacting With Others

People & Task Behavior

Another behavior to observe is <u>openness.</u> Openness is a person's willingness to show what's going on inside. Open people are very relationship and **people** oriented. In a sales situation, the open person will be asking questions and making statements that focus on the two of you and the relationship you are building.

The opposite of open is <u>self-contained</u>. The self-contained person is more **task** oriented and in a sales situation, asks mostly questions that deal with the subject at hand, wanting to deal with business first and get to know you later.

Open people are more flamboyant and outgoing. They draw attention to themselves. Self-Contained people tend not to draw attention to themselves.

The Four Basic Behavioral Styles

When you combine directness and openness behaviors on a grid, the four quadrants represent the four basic behavioral styles. This combination creates four basic patterns or styles of behavior: The Director(ruler), The Thinker(analyzer), The Relater(friend), and The Socializer(influencer).

The Director (Direct and Task Oriented)

Directors are self-contained, meaning task oriented, direct, and fast moving. They don't mind taking a bit of risk because they want forward motion. They want progress and achievements more than anything else. These people like to run things, they want to make their own decisions.

>   **STRENGTHS**
>   The strengths of a **Director** are directness and ability to get the job done quickly. The Director is blunt and quite assertive and therefore gets fast results. Diretors can generalize from details rather fast and see the big picture and the bottom line.
>
>   **WEAKNESSES**
>   The weaknesses of the **Director** grow out of the strengths. In that they can appear abrasive, insensitive to other people, and not concerned about details.

Interpreting the Four Styles When Interacting With Others

The Director (Direct and Task Oriented) Continued

GENERAL STRATEGIES
- Support their goals and objectives
- Keep your relationship businesslike.
- If you disagree, argue facts, not personal feelings.
- Give recognition to ideas-not the person
- To influence decisions, provide alternate actions and probabilities of their success.
- Be precise, efficient, time disciplined and well organized.

WHEN COMMUNICATING WITH THEM

PLAN to be prepared and organized, fast paced, and to the point.

MEET them in such a way that you get to the point quickly, keeping things professional and business like.

STUDY their goals and objectives, what they want to accomplish, what is happening now, and how they would like to see it changed.

PROPOSE solutions with clearly defined consequences and rewards that relate specifically to the Director's goals.

CONFIRM by providing two to three options, and let them make the decision.

ASSURE them that their time will not be wasted.

Overall Strategy: When you are communicating with Directors, they don't want you to say, "Here's what you should do." They want you to say, "Here are your options. What do you think?" Remember, they need to make the decisions. Same outcome, different process.

Goal: Be prepared to focus on "The Results."

Interpreting the Four Styles When Interacting With Others

The Thinker (Indirect and Task Oriented)

<u>Thinkers</u> are indirect people. Like Relaters, they tend to move at a slow pace. Thinkers are self-contained; they focus first on the task.

STRENGTHS

Thinkers tend to be precise, efficient, and well organized. They are task oriented and will persevere on what might otherwise be considered a boring task.

WEAKNESSES

Their weaknesses come from an extension of their strengths, in that they are often seen as too task oriented and too cool and impersonal. They are suspected of not being concerned about feelings because they place so much emphasis on facts. They may be perceived to be nit pickers who are such perfectionists, that they can't be effective.

GENERAL STRATEGIES
- Support their organized, thoughtful approach.
- Demonstrate through actions rather than words.
- Be systematic, exact, organized, and prepared.
- List advantages and disadvantages of any plan you propose.
- Give them time to verify your words and actions.
- Follow up your personal contacts with a letter.
- Provide solid, tangible, factual evidence that what you say is true and accurate.
- Do not rush the decision-making process.

WHEN COMMUNICATING WITH THEM

PLAN to be well prepared and equipped to answer all their questions.

MEET them cordially but get quickly to the task.

STUDY the situation in a practical, logical manner. Ask lots of questions and make sure your questions show a clear direction. The better your questions fit into the overall scheme of things, the more likely they are to give you the appropriate answers.

Interpreting the Four Styles When Interacting With Others

The Thinker (Indirect and Task Oriented) Continued
WHEN COMMUNICATING WITH THEM

> **PROPOSE** logical solutions to their problems. Document the how and the why, and show how your proposition is the logical thing to do.
>
> **CONFIRM** as a matter of course. Don't push; give them time to think. Offer documentation.
>
> **ASSURE** them through adequate service and follow-through. Be complete.

Overall Strategies: When you are communicating with a Thinker, you want to go slowly and focus on the business at hand. Cover the details, document your claims, go through each of the steps along the way. Don't skip over anything.

When you approach a Thinker, start by giving him or her an outline of what you are going to do. Explain your agenda, and then stick with it!! If you get off the agenda, the Thinker will notice.

Goal: Be prepared to justify the plan of action logically.

The Relater (Indirect and People Oriented)

Indirect and Open people are Relaters(friends).

Relaters like to maintain the status quo in their lives. They like their world just the way it is and are somewhat reluctant to make changes. If you propose a plan that requires major changes, they are likely to ask you to reconsider, or at least suggest a change that is not as radical.

> **STRENGTHS**
> The strengths of the Relater are warmth and the ability to build meaningful relationships with others. They are loyal and compliant. They are excellent team workers, willing to conform.
>
> **WEAKNESSES**
> Their weaknesses grow out of an extension of their strengths in that some people see them as too concerned about relationships to do an adequate job

Interpreting the Four Styles When Interacting With Others

The Relater (Indirect and People Oriented) Continued

of completing the task. Directors perceive them to be slow and ineffective. They are often so sensitive to the feelings and needs of others that they are unduly influenced by them.

GENERAL STRATEGIES
- Support their feelings
- Show personal interest
- When you disagree, discuss personal opinions and feelings
- Move along in an informal slow manner
- Show that you are "actively" listening
- Provide guarantees that any actions will involve a minimum of risk
- Offer personal assurances that you will stand behind any decisions.

WHEN COMMUNICATING WITH THEM

PLAN to get to know them personally. Be likable and nonthreatening, professional friendly.

MEET them by developing trust, friendship, and credibility. Go at a slow pace.

STUDY their feelings and emotional needs as well as their technical and business needs. Take time to get them to spell out what is really important to them.

PROPOSE by getting them involved. Show the human side of your proposal. Show how it affects them and their relationships withothers.

CONFIRM without pushing or rushing them. Provide personal assurances and guarantees wherever you can.

ASSURE by being consistent and regular in your communication.

<u>**Overall Strategy:**</u> When you are communicating with a <u>Relater</u>, recognize that major changes represent a threat to their established world and your plan is going to generate tension.
Goal: Be ready to reassure the Relater that everything is under control.

Interpreting the Four Styles When Interacting With Others

The Socializer (Direct and People Oriented)

<u>Socializers</u> are direct. They move quickly, they are open, and they focus on the relationship. They are playful and spontaneous. No matter what the situation, they've got a one-liner to slip in somewhere. Socializers love variety, they hate routine. They can't stand to follow the same schedule everyday-**it drives them wild.**

STRENGTHS

The strength of a Socializer lies in his or her enthusiasm and exciting playful nature. Socializers quickly win people over and get others caught up in their drive to accomplish a task. They are fun to be with and can adapt easily to a changing situation.

WEAKNESSES

The Socializer's weaknesses result from an extension of their strengths. They sometimes come on too strong and are seen as being artificial or "put on." Some times their playfulness and spontaneity is regarded as a lack of seriousness or as impracticability. They are not good detail people in that they are easily bored by anything that tends to be monotonous or has to be done alone.

GENERAL STRATEGIES
- Support opinions, ideas, and dreams
- Don't hurry the discussion
- Try not to argue
- Agree on the specifics of any agreement.
- Summarize in writing what you both agreed upon.
- Be entertaining and fast moving.
- Use testimonials to positively affect decisions.

WHEN COMMUNICATING WITH THEM

PLAN to be stimulating and interested in them. Allow them time to talk.

MEET them boldly; don't be shy. Introduce yourself first. Bring up new topics openly.

Interpreting the Four Styles When Interacting With Others

The Socializer (Direct and People Oriented) Continued

STUDY their dreams and goals as well as their other needs.

PROPOSE your solution with stories or illustrations that relate to them and their goals.

CONFIRM the details in writing. Be clear and direct.

ASSURE that they fully understand what they have brought and can demonstrate their ability to use it properly.

Overall Strategy: When you are communicating with **Socializers**, you want to be stimulating. Spend your time showing them the highlights and giving them the big picture. Do not focus on the little details.

Goal: Be flexible, be enthusiastic and let them talk. Be ready to provide them with "visual aids."

Lesson: Deal with people the way they want to be dealt with, not just the way you want to be dealt with.

The more we know about the four personality types, the better able we are to interact with them. As a result, we know how to approach them, how to deal with them, how to manage them, and how to be successful with them.

Refer to pages 23-25 of the LeaderSELF Assessment Inventory (LAI) and complete your answers to the categories on: Communication, Interacting with Impact, Managing Conflict, and Guiding Change.

Personal Listening Inventory

Take a few minutes to complete the following Personal Listening Inventory. Most of your answers will be on a scale of #1-#10 with 1 being low and 10 being high. However, item #2 asks you for a % from 0% to 100%. Think about a specific role you are fulfilling as you respond to the six items.

1. On a scale of 1-10 (with 10 being the highest), how commited are you to improving your listening? _____

2. On average, what percentage of each business day do you spend listening? _____

3. On a scale of 1-10, (with 10 being the highest), how would you rate yourself as a listener? _____

4. On a scale of 1-10, how would you rate the best listener you know? _____

5. On a scale of 1-10, how would you rate the worst listener you know? _____

6. On a scale of 1-10, (with 10 being the highest), how would the following people (where appropriate) rate you as a listener?

>   Manager _____   Spouse/Lover _____
>   Customer _____   Child(ren) _____
>   Close colleague _____ Best friend _____

Page Summary: Consider the following information as you review your answers.
Item #1: 8 or < communicates that you are committed to improving your listening.
Item #2: The average manager spends 60% of their day listening.
Item #3: Most people operate at about the 50% listening effectiveness level.
Item #4: The best listeners are at the top of the 10 point scale.
Item #5: The worst listeners are at the bottom of the 10 point scale.

Item #6: Our Managers usually rank us a bit higher than we rank ourselves. Does that mean that we actually listen to them better or pretend to listen better to them? Subordinate/Close Colleague usually rank us at the same level we rank ourselves. Spouse/Lover: By the way, this isn't an either or choice, my spouse ranks me a 0 and my lover ranks me a 10. Generally though, our spouse, lover, and/or kids rank us the lowest in our listening ability. Finally, our best friends rank us the highest. Why is that? A true best friend listens from the other person's point of view and empathizes.

Listening to Learn
Learning to Listen

Listening is the most used aspect of human communication.

In a typical workday:

*Managers and Supervisors...

--listen to superiors and subordinates in order to gather information for decision making and problem solving;

--listen to and mediate among differences and conflicts in staff opinions;

--interview and listen to prospective managers, staff, clients, and customers; and

--make presentations and listen to participants' comments and questions.

*Associates...

--listen to comments, announcements, and directions from managers and co-workers;

--listen to internal and external customers' comments, questions, complaints and compliments.

The opportunities for understanding or misunderstanding are countless. *So if people in an organization have poor listening skills, the costs may be high:*

*Wasted meeting time;
*Inaccurate orders, shipments and/or high returns;
*Lost sales opportunities; and
*Inadequately informed, misinformed, confused, or angry staff and customers.

Approximately 45% of all time spent communicating involves listening; next comes speaking with 30%, reading with 16%, and writing with 9%.

Levels of Listening

In looking at the graphic on empathic listening which appears on the next page, we can recognize that good listening is an active integrated communication skill that demands energy and know-how. It is purposeful, powerful and productive.

On the graphic, the key elements of communication are represented by the words: **Speaking, Observing and Hearing**. However, to communicate effectively we must also engage in an internal process of: **listening** (as a result of the other person speaking), **interpreting** (translating information which we selected through observing the speaker) and **evaluating** (giving meaning to our listening of the speaker's message).

Only after this internal process has been completed, can we respond appropriately.

> In "The Seven Habits of Effective People," bestselling author, Stephen Covey captures the challenges of listening within :
>
> **Habit #5: Seek First to Understand; Then to Be Understood.**
>
> *Seek first to understand involves a very deep shift in paradigm. We typically seek first to be understood.
>
> *Most people do not listen with the intent to understand; they listen with the intent to reply.

*When another person speaks, we are usually "listening" at one of four levels:

-**Ignoring**-not really listening at all, including lack of verbal/non-verbal cues;

-**Pretending**-not listening, however, providing verbal/non-verbal cues;

-**Selective/Attentive Listening**-listening only to what one "wants" to hear--whatever suits one's biases, isn't disturbing or challenging, and so on; usually involves attention to facts, but not to feelings. Spouses and managers/Associ ates often accuse one another of this;

-**Empathic Listening**-listening with intent to understand. Empathic listening gets inside another person's frame of reference. This involves listening to "put yourself in another person's place" to understand--but not necessarily agree with-what's being said and why.

Empathic Listening

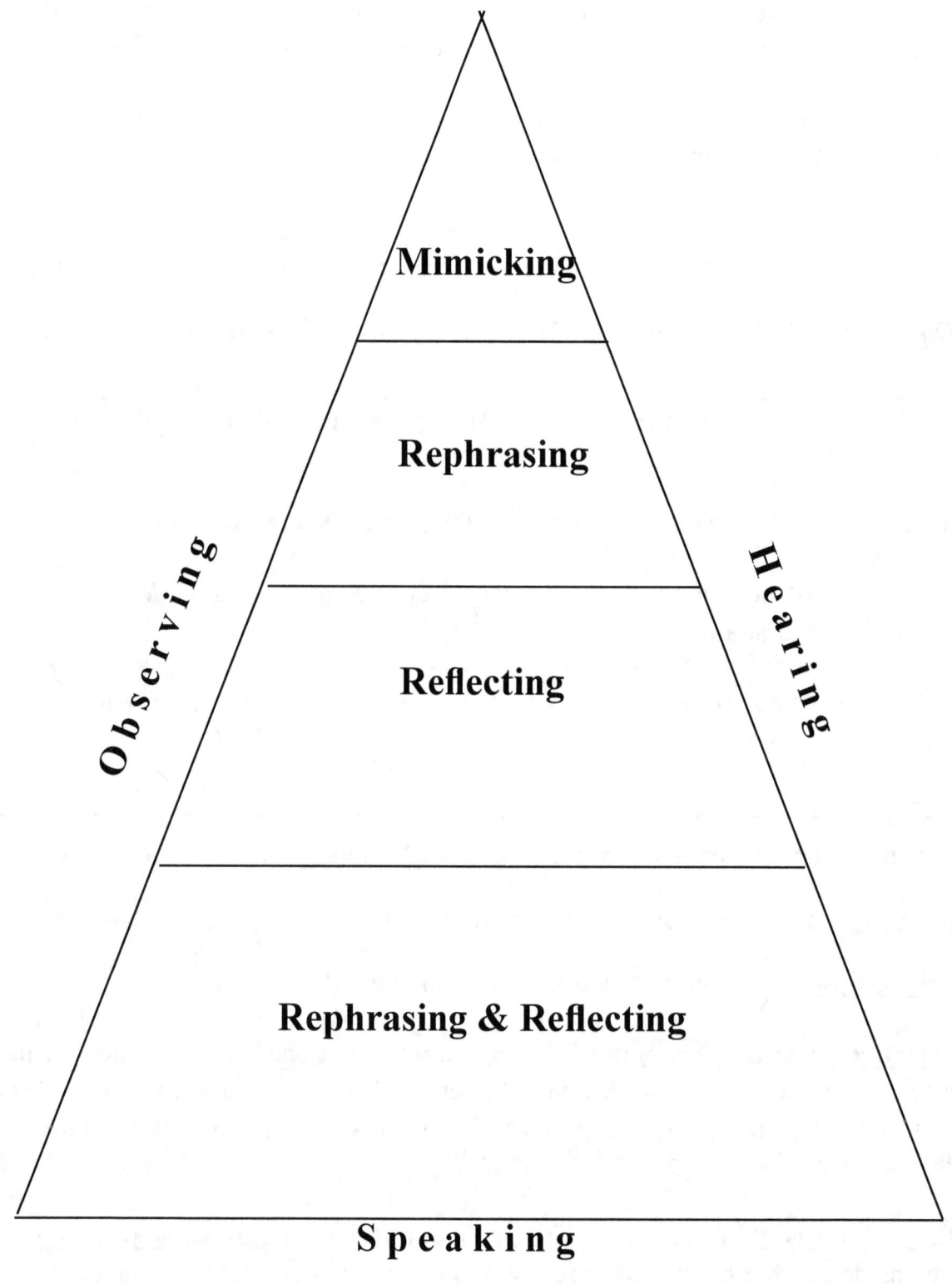

Empathic Listening
Four Developmental Stages

It is extremely difficult to say that you can truly understand another, without first, having had a similar direct experience or secondly, having made the commitment and taken the time to develop and practice empathic listening skills.

These skills involve the following four developmental stages:

Stage #1: The first and least effective stage is to **mimic content**. This is considered a first stage skill because it at least causes you to listen to what's being said. Mimicking content is easy. You just listen to the words that come out of someone's mouth and you repeat them. Team Leader: "I've had it! This performance management process is for the birds!" Manager: "You've had it. You think that the performance management process is for the birds."

You have essentially repeated back the content of what was being said. You haven't evaluated or probed or advised or interpreted. You've at least showed you're paying attention to his/her words. But to understand, you want to do more.

Stage #2: The second stage of empathic listening is to **rephrase the content**. It is a little more effective, but it is still limited to the verbal communication. Team Leader: "I've had it! This performance management process is for the birds!" Manager: "You don't want to deal with the performance management process anymore?"

This time you've put his/her meaning into your own words. Now you're thinking about what he/she said, mostly with the left side, the reasoning, logical side of the brain.

Stage #3: The third stage brings your right brain into operation. You **reflect feeling.** Team Leader: "I've had it! This performance management process is for the birds!" Manager: "You're really feeling frustrated with the performance management process." Frustration is the feeling; the performance management process is the content. You're using both sides of your brain to understand both sides of his/her communication.

Empathic Listening
Four Developmental Stages

Stage #4: Now, what happens when you use fourth stage empathic listening skills is really incredible. You authentically seek to understand, as you **rephrase content and reflect feeling**. In doing so, you also help him/her to work through their own thoughts and feelings. As he/she grows in confidence of your sincere desire to really listen and understand, the barrier between what's going on inside him/her and what's actually being communicated to you disappears. As a result, they are not thinking and feeling one thing and communicating another. They begin to trust you with their innermost tender feelings and thoughts.

Team Leader: "I've had it! The performance management process is for the birds!" (I want to talk with you, to get your attention.)
Manager: "You're really frustrated about the performance management process."
Team Leader's thought: (That's right! That's how I feel.)
Team Leader: "I sure am. It's totally impractical."
Manager: "You feel that there is no value in the performance management process."
Team Leader's thought: (Let me think--is that what I mean?)
Team Leader: "Well... I just don't understand how we can do our day to day job AND also the performance management process"
Manager: "You're not sure that our performance management process is practical."
Team Leader's thought: (Well....)
Team Leader: "Well, I guess we have to use some process to establish objectives and measure and monitor progress. But, how do we find the time to apply the performance objectives, performance factors and development plan to each of our staff and still accomplish our work as a team leader?"
Manager: How about if we set up a meeting with several colleagues and representatives from the Human Resources Department to discuss how we can more effectively implement the performance management process with our staff?

What a difference real understanding can make! All the well-meaning advice and opinion-giving in the world won't amount to anything if we're not addressing the real problem. And we'll never get to the real problem if we are so caught up in our own viewpoint, our own paradigms, that we don't hesitate for a moment to consider the situation from another point of view.

> **"Listening, really listening, is tough and grinding work, often humbling, sometimes distasteful."**

Feedback: A Critical Communication Skill (and Leadership Skill)

Management is Getting Results Through the Efforts of Others.

Getting Better Results Means Investing in People.

The Key to Developing People is Feedback.

Giving (and receiving) Feedback is a Basic Leadership Skill.

It Requires Honesty, Courage, Tact, and an Understanding and Respect for Others.

Understanding the Role of Feedback

When people act, they intend to achieve certain results. Without feedback they never know whether or not they are successful.

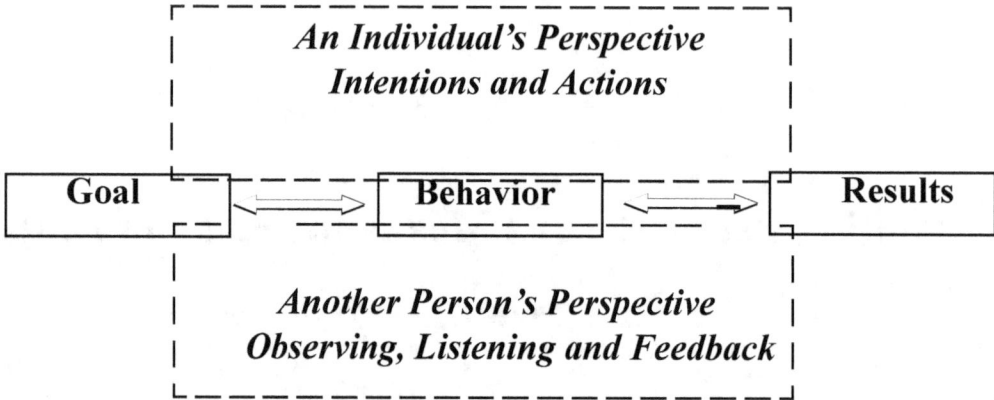

One of the most effective methods for human learning is <u>Reinforcement</u> and we use reinforcement techniques when we both provide feedback to others and seek feedback from others.

Feedback: A Bridge or Barrier to Understanding?

Feedback is the extent to which others are willing
to share and be open in providing
relevant information to the *individual*.

"Communication is a Joint Game Between the
Speaker and the Listener...
Against the Forces of Confusion."

Understanding the Value of Feedback: The Johari Window

The giving and receiving of feedback is the heart of effective communication, relationships and management. A framework to better understand the "dynamic" nature of feedback and it's impact on communication was developed by Joseph Luft and Harry Ingham. Their framework is called the Johari window and depicts attitudes and be-haviors that each individual engages in which relate to:

1. Areas Which Are Known to Self-This area includes those attitudes, behaviors and perceptions which are only know to the individual. It includes an understanding of the way they are coming across to others and the impact they may be having with the people they are attempting to influence.

2. Areas Which Are Unknown to Self-This area includes those attitudes, behaviors and perceptions which an individual may lack awareness of in regard to how they are coming across to others.

3. Areas Which are Known to Others- This area includes those personal and pro-fes-sional characteristics, attitudes, personality traits, roles, behaviors and perceptions which are know to others.

4. Areas Which are Unknown to Others- This area includes those personal and professional characteristics, attitudes, personality traits, roles, behaviors and perceptions which are unknown to others.

The Johari Window illustrates how **self-dislosure** and **feedback** contribute to effective communications.

Feedback: There are two processes that affect the shape of the Johari window. The first, which operates in the direction illustrated is called **feedback**. This is the extent to which others are willing to share and be open in providing relevant information (feedback) to the individual.

Disclosure: Another process which affects the shape of the Johari window is **disclosure.** This is the extent to which an individual is willing to share with others information about themselves. The most relevant disclosure is not what people say about themselves but rather their behavior. An interesting phenomenon occurs in settings where there is simultaneous feedback and disclosure as the area which was previously unknow to both self and others becomes known to both.

The Johari Window of Self

	Known to Self	**Unknown to Self**
Known to Others	Public	Blind
Unknown to Others	Private	Unknown

> The Johari Window provides an illustration of how self-dislosure and feedback contribute to effective communications at home, at work and at play.

Feedback Skills

Feedback, like most management skills, is an acquired behavior. Following are sug-gestions for improving a manager's feedback skills:

1. Give feedback directly. Associates who receive a manager's praise through a third party often regard the praise suspiciously and therefore don't act on it. As a result, the Associate may become insecure and distrustful.

2. Deliver feedback immediately. Give feedback as soon as possible after the event. Make sure you check out the appropriateness of the time and setting with the individual prior to providing feedback. Don't save feedback--whether good or bad--for the performance appraisal interview.

3. Be Specific. Effective feedback has an "I" component which says that "I observe..." or "I want to check out with you..." your behavior during a specific situation or with a specific individual. Generalized feedback has never led to improved perfor-mance.

4. Give feedback honestly. Feedback should only be given concerning behavior that the Associate has control over. Remember that Associates can "see through" superficial or condescending feedback.

5. Distribute feedback equally. The Leave Alone, Zap You (LAZY) model of feedback is ineffective. Under this approach, Associates receive no feedback until they do something wrong.

Giving and Receiving Feedback

When we **give feedback** to others we want to use self-disclosure techniques which allow us to share a part of our beliefs, values, attitudes and perceptions. However, in considering exactly what to disclose to others, keep in mind the appropriateness of the information that you want to share. When we **get feedback** from others we want to use probing and questioning techniques which are designed to elicit open-ended responses from an individual.

Interact With Impact: Some Challenges

The Interact with Impact segment of the LeaderSELF development program will provide you with clues for deciphering the difficult people in your life. Our approach uses the Personal Styles and Preferences concepts (Task/People/Direct/Indirect) and applies them to the strengths and weaknesses of each style preference. You will have an oppor-tunity to learn about the ten classic types of challenging people and their characteristics. You will also identify coping strategies for each challenging type of person, enhancing your ability to interact.

> The only person you can change is Yourself...
> You have two Choices...Change the Situation or...
> Change your Perception or Attitude of the Situation.

If you make up your mind that it is impossible to get along with everybody...then you are halfway there to proving yourself correct. You won't get along with everybody! In fact, until you make up your mind that **you can get along with everybody**...there will always be somebody you will think is difficult, challenging or impossible to get along

---

Three areas for determining what makes people challenging are:

1. **Behavior:** Visible, observable actions of individuals.
2. **Communication:** The strength of an individual's verbal, non-verbal, listening and feedback skills.
3. **Focus:** An individual's degree of attention to both the task and relationship aspects of interaction.

In order to relate to an individuals underlying needs, you need to develop **behavioral flexibility** -the ability to adapt your own behavior appropriately to meet the needs of the person you are dealing with.

Interact With Impact: Style Preferences

The Analyzer is competent, conservative, correct and conscientious. These are people who follow the rules and regulations. They achieve their goals through planning, education, and persistence. They are the detail people.

The Director is confident, direct, loves challenge and change, is willing to take charge and go for the action. These people don't wait for things to happen--they make them happen. Director personalities are often aggressive, self-motivated, goal-oriented and fast-moving.

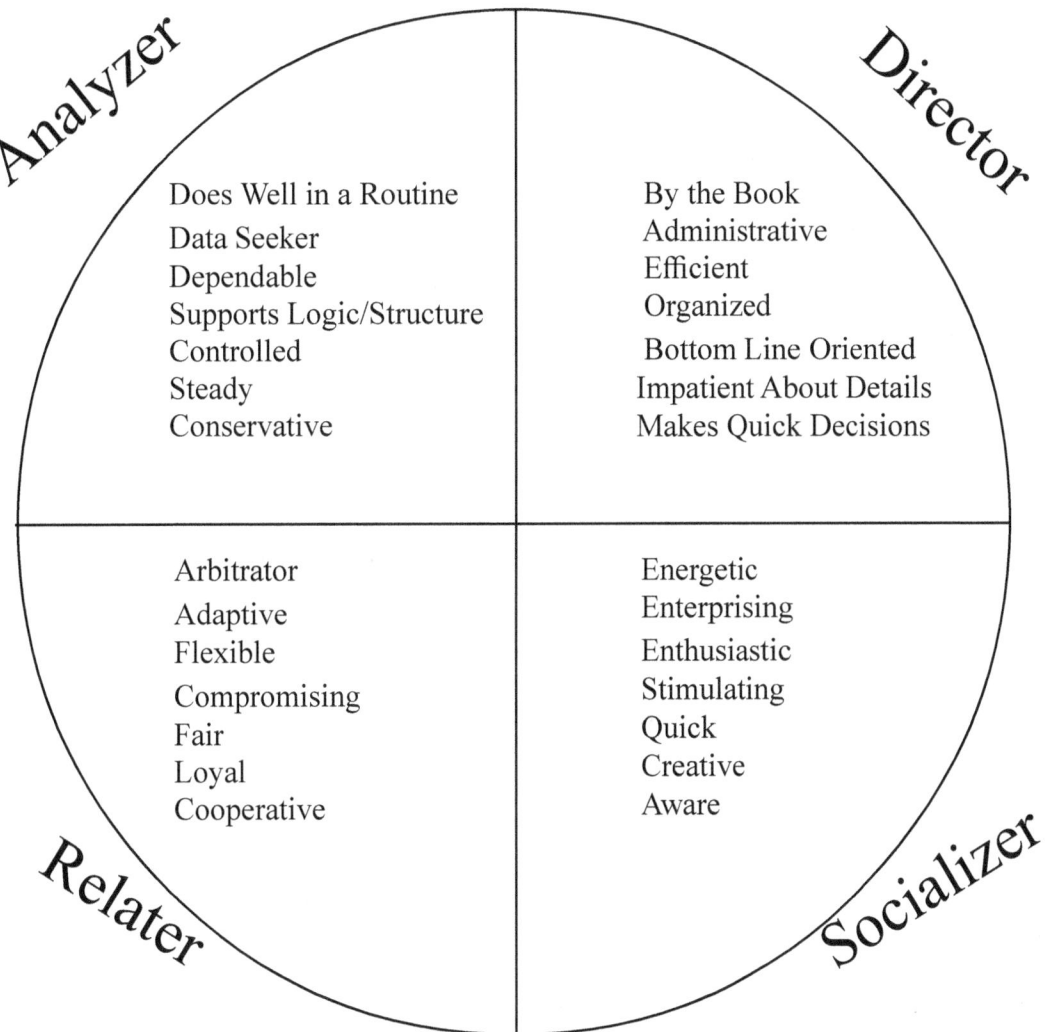

The Relater can get the job done and work harmoniously with a wide variety of people. They are good team players, and more and more companies are finding that those who succeed in business are Relaters. They are good listeners and prefer one-on-one conversations.

The Socializer is emotional, enthusiastic and tend to be disorganized. They are flexible and playful, and they go with the flow. They are open and outgoing, and enjoy working with people. They excel at motivating people.

Challenge: The Director

STRENGTHS

The strengths of a Director are directness and ability to get the job done quickly. The Director is blunt and quite assertive and therefore gets fast results. Directors can generalize from details rather fast and see the big picture and the bottom line.

WEAKNESSES

The weaknesses of the Director grow out of the strengths. They can appear to be abrasive, insensitive to other people, and not concerned about details. Some negative characteristics of a Director are that they can be rigid, stubborn, distant and critical.

GENERAL STRATEGIES

Support their goals and objectives
Keep your relationship businesslike.

If you disagree, argue facts, not personal feelings.
Give recognition to ideas-not the person
To influence decisions, provide alternate actions and probabilities of their success.
Be precise, efficient, time disciplined and well organized.

WHEN COMMUNICATING WITH THEM

PLAN to be prepared and organized, fast paced, and to the point.

MEET them in such a way that you get to the point quickly, keeping things professional and businesslike.

STUDY their goals and objectives, what they want to accomplish, what is happening now, and how they would like to see it changed.

PROPOSE solutions with clearly defined consequences and rewards that relate specifically to their goals.

CONFIRM by providing two to three options, and let them make the decision.

ASSURE them that their time will not be wanted. After the sale confirm that the proposals you suggested did in fact provide the bottom line results expected.

Challenge: The Analyzer

Think About It

STRENGTHS

Thinkers tend to be precise, efficient, and well organized. They are task oriented and will persevere on what might otherwise be considered a boring task. They are thorough and meticulous and have high-standards.

WEAKNESSES

Their weaknesses come from an extension of their strengths, in that they are often seen as too task oriented and too cool and impersonal. They are sus-pected of not being concerned about feelings because they place so much emphasis on facts.

GENERAL STRATEGIES

Support their organized, thoughtful approach.
Be systematic, exact, organized, and prepared.
List advantaages and disadvantages of any plan.
Give them time to verify your words and actions.
Do not rush the decision-making process.
Provide solid, tangible, factual evidence that what you say is true and accurate.

WHEN COMMUNICATING WITH THEM

PLAN to be well prepared and equipped to answer all their questions.

MEET them cordially but get quickly to the task.

STUDY the situation in a practical, logical manner. Ask lots of questions and make sure your questions show a clear direction. The better your questions fit into the overall scheme of things, the more likely they are to give you the appropriate answers.

PROPOSE logical solutions to their problems. Document the how and the why, and show how your proposition is the logical thing to do.

CONFIRM as a matter of course. Don't push; give them time to think. Offer documentation.

ASSURE them through adequate service and follow-through. Be complete.

Challenge: The Relater

STRENGTHS
The strengths of the Relater are warmth and the ability to build meaningful relationships with others. They are loyal and compliant. They are excellent team workers, willing to conform.

With Your Friends

WEAKNESSES
Their weaknesses grow out of an extension of their strengths in that some people see them as too concerned about relationships to do an adequate job of completing the task. They are often so sensitive to the feelings and needs of others that they are unduly influenced by them.

GENERAL STRATEGIES

*Show personal interest
*Support their feelings
*Show that you are "actively" listening
*When you disagree, discuss personal opinions and feelings
*Move along in an informal slow manner
*Provide guarantees that any actions will involve minimum risk
*Offer personal assurances that you will support their decisions.

WHEN COMMUNICATING WITH THEM

PLAN to get to know them personally. Be likable and nonthreatening, professional friendly.

MEET them by developing trust, friendship, and credibility. Go at a slow pace.

STUDY their feelings and emotional needs as well as their technical and business needs. Take time to get them to spell out what is really important to them.

PROPOSE by getting them involved. Show the human side of your proposal. Show how it affects them and their relationships with others.

CONFIRM without pushing or rushing them. Provide personal assurances and guarantees wherever you can.

ASSURE by being consistent and regular in your communication. Give them the nurturing and reassurance that you would give someone who has highly concerned about the purchase they had just made.

Challenge: The Socializer

STRENGTHS

The strength of a Socializer lies in his or her enthusiasm and exciting playful nature. Socializers quickly win people over and get others caught up in their drive to accomplish a task. They are fun to be with and can adapt easily to a changing situation. They always have something to say regardless of what the topic may be, and they usually say it in an interesting way.

WEAKNESSES

The Socializer's weaknesses result from an extension of their strengths. They sometimes come on too strong and are seen as being artificial or "put on." Sometimes their playfulness and spontaneity is regarded as a lack of seriousness. They are easily bored by anything that is monotonous or has to be done alone.

GENERAL STRATEGIES

Support opinions, ideas, and dreams
Don't hurry the discussion
Try not to argue
Agree on the specifics of any agreement.
Summarize in writing what you both agreed upon.
Be entertaining and fast moving.
Use testimonials to positively affect decisions.

WHEN COMMUNICATING WITH THEM

PLAN to be stimulating and interested in them. Allow them time to talk.

MEET them boldly; don't be shy. Introduce yourself first. Bring up new topics openly.

STUDY their dreams and goals as well as their other needs.

PROPOSE your solution with stories or illustrations that relate to them and their goals.

CONFIRM the details in writing. Be clear and direct.

ASSURE that they fully understand what they have bought and can demonstrate their ability to use it properly.

The Ten Classic Types of Challenging People

> **For Every Behavior...There is a Stimulus and a Response.
> The Individual Provides the Stimulus and You Provide the Response.**

1. The Bull (or Sherman Tank): This type of individual attempts to intimidate and control through aggressiveness. Bulls possess tremendous power in interpersonal situations. Such power comes largely from the typical responses their behavior arouses: confusion, mental or physical flight, or a sense of helpless frustration that leads to tears or tantrumlike rage.

<u>Characteristics:</u>   Stress behavior of the **Director**
    They become irrational in their thinking and in their behavior
    They will have the last word..."one last sentence"...

<u>Reason for behavior:</u> They perceive that they have lost control and they aren't getting results.
    "Read My Lips"=Regaining Control

Results: Bulls usually achieve their short-term objectives, but they do so at the cost of honest disagreement from others, lost friendships, and the long-term erosion of relationships with their co-workers.

2. The Fox (or Sniper): This type of individual attempts to attack others through the use of sly verbal assaults. The chosen recipients are struck by well-placed verbal missiles, high-powered enough to hurt. But the attack is accompanied by nonverbal signals that say "Pretend that what I'm doing is nice and neutral, or that you don't even hear me."

Characteristics; Stress behavior of the **Sociaizer**
    Skillful use of Sarcasm
    Humorous delivery of the"dart in the back."

<u>Reason for behavior:</u> They, like The Bull, have a very strong sense of how others ought to think and act. They often have firm views of what can be done to solve the problems that interfere with their own personal goals. However, since their "I'm superior" orientation tends to interfere with seeing things from others' perspectives, what Foxes expect from a boss, co-worker, or spouse is often unrealistic.

<u>Results:</u> The cycle is a sad one. The Fox behavior is often a response to an unresolved or unheeded problem. The unresolved problems continue or become worse, and the resulting stress produces more difficult behavior. This self-destructive cycle will continue until the victim decides to stop being a victim, thus changing the nature of the interaction.

The Ten Classic Types of Challenging People

3. The Time Bomb (or Exploder): This type of individual displays Hostile-Aggressive behavior in the form of an adult tantrum, which can be described as a fearsome attack filled with range that seems barely under control. It is particularly unnerving that such behavior often erupts during a discussion that appeared at the start to be friendly and reasonable.

Characteristics: Stress behavior of the **Relater**
An individual may "Give, Give & Give" and then explode!
To those who have them, tantrums happen, they are not planned.

Reason for behavior: An adult tantrum is a sudden, almost automatic response to a situation in which a person feels both thwarted and psychologically threatened. Frequently, the very fact that something is seen as threatening is outside the awareness of both parties. When sparked in some way, the Time Bomb feels first angry and then blaming or suspicious.

Results: Time Bombs appear more out of control of themselves than Bulls or Foxes. While observers may talk of Bulls and Foxes as mean, vicious, or terrifying, they more often use such words as "over-emotional," "super-touchy," and "irritable" to describe Time Bombs.

4. The Whiner (or Complainer): This type of individual finds fault with everything, malcontents who gripe ad nauseam about everything from how messy your desk is to the temperature outside. The disguised message behind all the gripes is that "someone," usually meaning you, should be doing something about them. Whiners should not be confused with people who have a legitimate complaint and are simply trying to bring it to someone's attention, or with those individuals who just need to get something off their chests.

Characteristics: Stress behavior of the **Relater** "And another thing..." is often heard out of their mouths.
"Triangular Complainer/Whiners" are a breed who don't complain at you, they complain to you about other terrible people.

Reason for behavior: Complainers fall into that group that feels powerless in the management of their own lives, as if the causes of all that happens to them lie outside their grasp. From this pas-sive view, all that goes well can be attributed to good luck or to favors from benevolent others. Effort, ingenuity, and ability are, in this light, without significant power to affect anything.

Results: While Complainers do get attention, they seldom get action. Impatience, patronizing dismissal, oversolicitous personal attention, or simply avoidance are more often their lot.

The Ten Classic Types of Challenging People

5. The Stone Wall (or The Clam): This type of individual displays Passive-Aggressive behavior by doing absolutely nothing! Did you ever have to deal with someone who won't talk? They just sit there and stare at you no matter what you say. They give people "the silent treatment." The perplexing thing about Clams is that there are so many varieties of them. All of them, however, learned unresponsiveness in general because it provides a number of short-run benefits.

<u>Characteristics:</u>   Stress behavior of a **Director or Analyzer**
    They react to a probe or disagreeable situation by closing down
    Silent and unresponsive

<u>Reason for behavior:</u>   For some, responsiveness is a noncommittal way of handling potentially painful interpersonal situations
    For others, the charm of silence is calculated aggression
    And, for some, clamming up is a way of evading themselves because spoken words give concrete meaning to thoughts and feelings

<u>Results:</u> Nonverbal cues are seldom sufficient to deduce the nature of the silent beast you're confronting. As a result, it is often necessary to understand what the silence or lack of response means.

6. The Ultra or Super Agreeable: Ultra Agreeables always have a smile and a friendly word for you. Best of all, they seem so responsive. Whatever you want from them, you get. What neat, sweet people, UNTIL you need some action. They always tell you things that are satisfying to hear. But, they are challenging, because they leave you believing they are in agreement with your plans, only to let you down.

<u>Characteristics:</u>   Stress behavior of a **Relater**
    They YES you to death!
    Super Agreeables often make unrealistic commitments

<u>Reason for behavior:</u> They need to be liked or at least accepted by every single person all of the time. They do not feel accepted. They don't tell you how they really feel because they are afraid you won't like them.

<u>Results:</u> The Super Agreeable's avoidance of conflict has some short-term benefits, but these are gained at a long-term high cost. The tragedy is that if Super Agreeables were straight-forward to begin with, and they and you could put up with some minor unpleasantries, the problem could more easily be resolved and much bad feeling could be avoided.

The Ten Classic Types of Challenging People

7. The Negativist (or The Wet Blanket): This type of individual is convinced that they have little power over their own lives. Fate, in the form of overpowering natural or manmade forces, intervenes at every front, never completely within anyone's power to contain. Because Negativists truly feel dispirited and defeated, their pessimistic comments can easily arouse resonant feelings in friends, family or colleagues.

Characteristics:
- Stress behavior of an **Analyzer**
- They have a need for everything they do and everything in their environment to be perfect.
- They use comments such as: "There's nothing we can do," "It won't work," "We tried that last year," and "Forget it, they'll never let us do it."

Reason for behavior: Negativists, like Complainers, are convinced that they have little power over their own lives. To understand Negativists, it is important to realize that they are not by intention obstructionists to every scheme. They, in truth, believe that the blocking forces are out of their, or any ordinary person's control.

Results: Negativists are not aware that they have an underlying loss of faith in the future. They see instead a constant flow of reasons why life events cannot be dealt with in a positive way. To make sense of this pessimistic view, they support it with the best rationality they can muster. Small wonder that they become irritated with you when you persist in thinking that something might yet be done to save the situation.

8. The Know-It-All (or Bulldozer): This type of individual conveys a belief in their own superiority that often leaves us imperfect earthlings feeling humiliated, immobilized, and helplessly angry. The Know-It-All is a highly productive person, a thorough and accurate thinker who makes competent, careful plans and then carries them through, even when obstacles are great.

Characteristics:
- Stress behavior of a **Director** There is a tone of absolute certainty
- Bulldozers leave little room for anyone else's judgments, creativity or resourcefulness

Reason for behavior: Know-It-Alls believe that all of the forces that shape them are in their direct control. Their early life experiences led to their construction of a world in which they always got what they deserved. Unequivocal praise or blame from parents plus a sense of their own ability to affect things by careful planning and follow-through led easily to the belief that if good or bad things happen, they, not fate or luck, are the cause.

The Ten Classic Types of Challenging People

9. The Phony Know-It-Alls (or Balloons): This type of individual speaks with great authority about subjects of which they have little knowledge, and even that little knowledge may be inaccu-rate. The term Balloon is used to describe them because the definition of balloon is " an object with thin flexible walls filled with hot air or gas." Balloons are often very curious people. They read newspapers, browse through the first four chapters of many books, listen hard to the rumor mill and eavesdrop wherever they can. What a great way to acquire scraps and bits of knowledge about lots of interesting things.

Characteristics: Stress behavior of a **Socializer** They will "be" whoever they are with.

This type of individual typically doesn't know everything...but they can talk about whatever you want to talk about...even if they don't know what you are talking about!

Reason for behavior: At the heart of the Balloon's motivation seems to be the overwhelming desire to be admired and respected by others. Not so much to be liked as to be thought well of and seen as a person of importance.

Results: Interactions often go like this:
1. I want them to see how competent I am
2. What I'm thinking sounds so plausible, it's probably true
3. If it is true, why not say so
4. Well, nobody has called me a liar, so I guess it was true
5. Now, I know I'm competent.

10. The Procrastinator (or Staller): This type of individual can't make up their minds so they have a tendency to stall off major decisions until they go away. Stallers become challenging individuals when something in your own life depends on their taking action. But Stallers do not simply prolong the decision making process, they avoid it, sometimes to absurd and unproductive limits.

Characteristics: **Any style can procrastinate, but Relater's and Analyzer's** seem to have this tendency.

Stallers often use this line of thinking: "However I decide, someone will not like it. I cannot knowingly and directly hurt anyone. What am I to do?"

Reason for behavior: Super Agreeables and Stallers both leave you believing they are in agreement with your plans, only to let you down. Super Agreeables can't tell you no because they fear the loss of your approval. Stallers, by contrast, can't reach a decision because they can't bear to

Matching Challenging People and Their Characteristics (See p 99) (Type)

Circle One...   (Characteristics) Circle One...

1. The Bull (or Sherman Tank)   1. They close down
                                      1. Silent and unresponsive

2. The Fox (or Sniper)   2. "And another thing..."
                                      2. Powerless in managing self

3. The Time Bomb (or Exploder)   3. Skillful use of sarcasm
                                      3. How others ought to think

4. The Whiner (or Complainer)   4. Give's & give's and then explodes
                                      4. Responds to perceived threats

5. The Stone Wall (or The Clam)   5. "Read My Lips"...
                                      5. Irrational in thinking & behavior

6. The Ultra (or Super Agreeable)   6. "What am I to do?"
                                      6. "There's no need to decide."

7. The Negativist (or Wet Blanket)   7. They can "be" who they are with
                                      7. Desires to be admired by others

8. The Know-It-All (or Bulldozer)   8. Need for perfection
                                      8. "There's nothing we can do."

9. The Phony Know-It-All (or Balloon) 9. Tone of absolute certainty
                                      9. Little room for anyone else

10. The Procrastinator (or Staller)   10. They YES you to death
                                      10. Make unrealistic commitments

Matching Stress Behavior and Coping Strategies of the Ten Challenging Types (See p 99)

(Stress Behavior of) Circle One...   (Coping Strategies) Circle One...

1. Relater and Analyzer

1. You must work hard to surface the underlying facts and issues that prevent this individual from taking action.

2. Socializer

2. Stand up for yourself without fighting and don't worry about being polite, just get in any way you can.

3. Director

3. State correct facts or alternative opinions as your own perceptions of reality.

4. Analyzer

4. Try to move to a problem-solving mode by asking specific, informational questions.

5. Relater

5. Surface the attack by smoking them out and provide an alternative to a direct contest

6. Director or Analyzer

6. Listen carefully and paraphrase back the main points of this individual's proposals

7. Relater

7. Make optimistic but realistic statements about past successes in solving similar problems.

8. Relater

8. Listen for indirect words, hesitations, and omissions that may provide clues to problem areas.

9. Socializer

9. Get agreement on or state clearly how much time is set aside for your "conversation."

10. Director

10. Give them time to run down and regain self-control on their own. Show that you take them seriously.

The Answer Key for Matching Stress Behavior and Coping Strategies

Type	Characteristics	Stress Behavior	Coping Strategy
1. The Bull	5. "Read My Lips"...	10. Director	2. Stand up for yourself
2. The Fox	3. Skillful us of scarcasm	9. Socializer	5. Surface the attack...
3. The Time Bomb	4. Gives & gives	8. Relater	10. Give them time...
4. The Whiner	2. And another thing...	7. Relater	4. Try to move to problem solving...
5. The Stone Wall	1. They close down...	6. Director or Analyzer	9. Get aggreement...
6. The Ultra Agreeable	10. They yes you...	5. Relater	1. You must work...
7. The Negativist	8. Need for perfection	4. Analyzer	7. Make optimistic...
8. The Know-It-All	9. Tone of absolute certainty	3. Director	6. Listen carefully and paraphrase...
9. The Phony Know-It-All	7. They can "be" who they are with...	2. Socializer	3. State correct facts...
10. The Procrastinator	6. What am I to do?	1. Relater and Analyzer	8. Listen for indirect words...

Coping Strategies: The Basic Six Steps

1st: Assess the Situation: Determine whether or not you are dealing with a Difficult Person or with a situation that is temporarily bringing out the worst in an ordinarily nondifficult person.

2nd: Stop wishing they were different...It is with others as they are that you must learn to cope.

3rd: Get some **distance** between you and the difficult behavior...Difficult people are difficult to us because they touch off a series of reactions in ourselves which always seem to become part of their game. (Imagine distancing them, their voice from you, or labeling them (indecisive, complainer) so you can better concentrate on coping with them).

4th: Formulate a plan for coping/interrupting the interaction...The basic tenet that underlies successful coping is a simple but often overlooked fact: THE BEHAVIOR OF HUMAN BEINGS IS HIGHLY INTERACTIONAL. Put another way: There is always a relationship between an individual's personality and the specific situation the person is in, *as the person sees it.*

5th: Implement your strategy...Timing is critical...First, you should select a period when the Difficult Person is not overburdened with other problems. Second, is whether or not you have the time yourself, and the energy, to carry through with your coping plan.

6th: Monitor the progress of your coping strategy and modify when appropriate. Expect to have to persist, plan and become as skillful as you can, because you may be the only one supplying the energy and motivation.

---

*Two Cycles of Behavior:

Negative Interaction Cycle: An initial negative encounter between two individuals spirals into increasingly negative and unproductive interactions.

Positive Interaction Cycle: The interaction between two individuals cycled in a positive direction.

Coping Strategies: The Time Bomb & The Fox

The Time Bomb

1. Don't use fighting words like "You're wrong." Do say things like "In my opinion..." or "I don't agree with you but I want to hear more of what you're saying.

2. Use the persons name at the beginning of the conversation or whenever you want to take control.

3. Keep eye contact at all times.

4. Let him/her explode until they have run out of powder.

5. Stop the Time Bomb from interrupting you by telling him "You interrupted me," then continue with what you were sayng. Each time he/she interrupts, you must stop them with the same sentence, "You interrupted me." If you allow them to interrupt you, they will see you as weak.

6. Don't take the Time Bombs attacks personally.

7. Make sure that your communication is at eye level, either sitting or standing. Don't stay seated when he/she is standing over you.

> Once you have dealt appropriately with the Time Bomb, he/she will have a new respect for you.

The Fox

1. Bring the sarcasm out into the open.

2. Question for intent.

3. Don't act vulnerable.

4. Find out the hidden agenda. Is the attacker jealous or angry?

5. Respond only to the compliment part of the sarcasm, not the put-down.

6. Realize that this person is not going to change. Do not give him or her the benefit of the doubt.

7. Do move on to solve any problems that are uncovered.

> Learn to recognize hurtful sarcasm immediately and respond (not react) to keep it out in the open and away from you.

Coping Strategies: The Bull & The Whiner

The Bull

1. Only respond to the actual facts of the situation.

2. Stay calm. Never respond with hostility.

3. Think about why this person needs to put you down. Once you can understand his underlying reasons, you will be able to respond in a more productive manner. This doesn't mean that you will like his behavior, but if you do understand it and continue to stay calm, it is quite possible that he will begin to change.

4. Ask questions: "Why would you say that?" or "Could you explain?"

5. Leave the situation (if possible).

6. Let the Bull know you will not be a victim of his or her attacks.

7. Watch your body language, keep eye contact, show self-confidence.

8. Don't get hooked by acting on your anger.

> The basic strategy for the verbal attack is to respond to the presumption, not the insult ie:
> Attack: Any fool knows that this is the wrong way to report these numbers.
> (Presumes the victim is a fool).
> Response: I'm sorry you feel I'm foolish. How would you like the numbers reported?"

The Whiner

1. Don't fall for their whining. Try: "I have heard that before, what are you going to do about it?"

2. Let the Whiner know that he or she cannot bring you a problem without a potential solution.

3. Discover what the "real problem" is. Be careful: Do not encourage more whining.

4. Make the whiner responsible. Don't fix things for this person. Create a situation where the individual is "response-able" or able to take the responsibility to respond.

5. Get the Whiner to write a list of all his or her worries, and next to each worry, how he or she will deal with it. This may help to separate worries from concerns. It is understandable that individuals might be concerned about certain situations and issues. However, it is counterproductive for an individual to take a "worst case scenario" approach to ALL of their concerns through constant WORRY, WORRY, WORRY.

6. Don't imagine this behavior will change on its own.

Coping Strategies: The Stone Wall & Ultra Agreeable

The Stone Wall

1. The most important thing for you to do when dealing with the Stone Wall is to get them to talk.

2. Watch his or her body language in order to get some feedback on how he or she is feeling.

3. Ask open-ended questions to encourage communication with questions such as the following: How do you feel about that? What is your opinion of this? or What is your reaction to this situation?

4. You **must** be silent after asking a question or making a statement. Do not speak, no matter how long it takes the Stone Wall to respond to your question.

5. Take control of the silence. Don't look threatening by staring or frowning. Instead look inquisitive, eyes wide open.

6. When the Stone Wall does respond, allow the person to carry on the conversation as long as possible.

7. Do not interrupt. When you do speak again, support the communication by asking another pertinent open-ended question in order to keep him or her involved.

The Ultra Agreeable

1. You must work hard to surface the underlying facts and issues that prevent the Ultra Agreeables from taking action.

2. Let them know that you value them as people by telling them directly, asking or remarking about family, hobbies, wearing apparel. Do this only if you mean it.

3. Ask them to tell you about those things that might interfere with your good relationship.

4. Ask them to talk about any aspect of your product, service, or self (if appropriate, only) that is not as good as the best.

5. Be ready to compromise and negotiate if open conflict is in the wind.

6. Listen to a Super-Agreeable's humor. Ther may be hidden messages in those quips or teasing remarks.

Coping Strategies: The Negativist and The Know-It-All

The Negativist

1. Be alert to the potential, in yourself and others, for being dragged down into despair.

2. Make optimistic but realistic statements about past successes in solving similar problems.

3. Don't try to argue Negativists out of their pessimism.

4. Do not offer solution-alternatives yourself until the problem has been thoroughly discussed.

5. When an alternative solution is being seriously considered, quickly raise the question yourself of negative events that might occur if the alternative were implemented.

6. See the doomsayings of the Negativist in perspective as potential problems to be overcome.

7. Be ready to take action on your own. Announce your plans to do this without equivocation.

8. Beware of eliciting negativistic responses from analytical people by asking them to act before they feel ready.

The Know-It-All

1. Be prepared.

2. Listen Carefuly.

3. Don't make mistakes.

4. Double-check all your work and facts. This type of difficult person is influenced by facts.

5. Give him/her all the power she wants. Let him/her know that you feel he/she has all the right answers and that you are willing to let him/her run the show.

6. Ask specific questions based on your knowledge and research of the issue.

7. Don't challenge, but offer alternative ideas if you know he/she is wrong.

8. Let him/her save face is he/she is wrong.

9. Make friends, not enemies.

Coping Strategies: The Phony Know-It-All and The Procrastinator

The Phony Know-It-All

1. Ask Questions. Get them to elaborate. Remember that he/she is all headlines and no news and therefore he/she will soon run out of back-up information.

2. Blow his cover if you are an expert, but be aware that he/she may go on the attack.

3. Cope with him alone.

4. Point out that his opinions may not be accurate, while leaving his giant-size ego intact.

5. Correct him in a meeting only when you have no other choice. Be gentle and move on to another topic.

6. Decide if it is worth your time to be with this person.

The Procrastinator

1. Make it easy for Procrastinators to tell you about conflicts or reservations that prevent the decision.

2. Listen for indirect words, hesitations, and omissions that may provide clues to problem areas.

3. When you have surfaced the issues, help Procrastinator's solve their problems with the decision.

4. At times the Procrastinator's reservation will be about you.
   If so... 1st: Acknowledge any past problem,

   2nd: State relevant data nondefensively,

   3rd: Propose a plan,

   4th: Ask for their help in resolving issue.

5. If you are not part of the problem, concentrate on helping the Procrastinator examine facts. Use the facts to place alternative solutions in priority order.

6. Give support after the decision seems to have been made.

7. If possible, keep the action steps in your hands.

Influencing Others

Chapter Five

Principle #4: Influencing Others (team and organizational focus)

> Research has shown that people conceive of success on a job as relating to three things:
>
> 1. The ability to contribute their ideas or suggestions,
> 2. The idea that their supervisor (leader) was listening to what they had to say, and
> 3. The possibility that their ideas and suggestions were put into action.
>
> As leaders, each one of us has an opportunity to create a work environment that respects and values constituent involvement and collaboration in decision-making. This type of work environment enhances constituent morale, motivation and commitment.

To create a work environment such as the one depicted above, a leader needs to demon-strate the ability to create and sustain interpersonal relationships. Additionally, effective leaders know the importance of building consensus through high levels of interaction, mutual exchange and collaboration, creating an environment neutralizing the potential for "power over" relationships.

The central tenents found within this type of work environment are equality and empowerment. By equality, we mean each constituent's mutual opportunity to influence one another without reference to status or prestige. And, by empowerment, we mean each constituent's ability to be accountable for some action because she has accepted both the responsibility and authority to act.

> Shared vision, communication, constituent leadership and teamwork provide a "formula for success" for building commitment to personal and organizational success.

Creating a Non-Threatening Environment

$$Behavior = f(I + E)$$

All Behavior is Learned. Let's examine the above formula: **Behavior = f (I + E)**. The **Behavior** (visible observable actions) we detect in the workplace are the result or function of the **Individual** and the **Environment** within which the individual performs. One of the most important roles of a leader is to create a work environment within which people are free to participate, grow and develop while contributing to the growth and development of the organization.

Take a few minutes to reflect on this formula and answer the following statement: "The work environment I'd like to create is one where Associates/Constituents will: _____.
Hopefully, your statement communicates a willingness to build consensus through high levels of constituent acceptance, participation, involvement and contribution.

Non-Acceptance Involves	Acceptance Involves
•Criticisms	•Listening
•Unfair comparisons	•Accepting another's ideas
•Avoidance	•Sharing information
•Advice-Giving	•Showing interest in others
•Rejection of the other's ideas	•Expressing appreciation

Individual Activity: In striving to create a non-threatening environment, why would it be important to avoid displaying behavior described within the left-hand column? (Answer: Non-acceptance behavior results in antagonistic feelings, non-cooperation, hos-tility and disinterest). What are some outcomes that the acceptance of others, provide? (Answer: Acceptance behavior results in high levels of rapport, respect, cooperation,and high morale.)

Inspiring Shared Vision

"Vision Without Action, Is Just a Dream.
Action Without Vision, Just Passes the Time.
But, Vision and Action, Can Change the World."

Joel Barker

Vision, a compelling view of a future yet to be, creates meaning and purpose which catapults both individuals and organizations to high levels of achievement. We create meaning in our lives by pursuing our future visions, and we refine our visions based on the meaning we are discovering through our experience. In examining Joel Barker's quote above, in regard to the power of vision, it can be realized that within organizations, vision can be utilized to empower individuals to "take action" to realize high levels of contribution and achievement.

The ongoing task of organizational leadership is to articulate and nurture a shared vision that engages and empowers individuals in order to bring out the best in people. It's the most inspiring future you can imagine. Because of this, you can never truly achieve your vision. You work toward it. Your vision communicates to others who you are and who you want to become—not what you have achieved.

Personal Visions are the Foundation for A Shared Vision

Creating Your Personal Vision: Prior to creating a shared vision, constituents should be encouraged to complete the Visioning Activity on pages 30-31. This information will serve as the foundation for determining key components of a shared organizational vision.

"Aligning" Constitutents around a Shared Vision: Organizational time should be scheduled to assemble constituents to share each of their personal visions. This process can be facilitated through small group discussions of 6-10 constituents engaging in a "dialogue." Each person should have an opportunity to share their information from pages 30-31. A "recorder" should take notes in order to "capture" highlights of each constituents personal vision. After each person has shared their information, constitutents from each small group should review all visions and identify "key" words or themes for "a shared vision." Each small group will then take turns presenting their shared vision words and themes. A recorder should take notes reflecting all of the small group contri-butions. This information should be assembled into a document and distributed to all constituents for additional input. Constituent feedback should be used for the leader-ship team to draft a shared vision statement for final constituent review and feedback.

Encouraging Constituent Leadership: Developing Others

From Reactive to Proactive: The Empowerment Continuum

I define leadership as "an influence relationship between two or more individuals." By influence, I mean that an individual can have an effect upon another without apparent exertion of force or direct exercise of command. By demonstrating leadership in this fashion, constituents engage in influence without authority. Influencing others without exhibiting authority is a significant characteristic of the LeaderSELF model because the process transcends an individual's role and title. And, because constitutents can influence others, they can all demonstrate leadership behavior or "constituent leadership." Effective leaders can facilitate constituent leadership according to the following continuum.

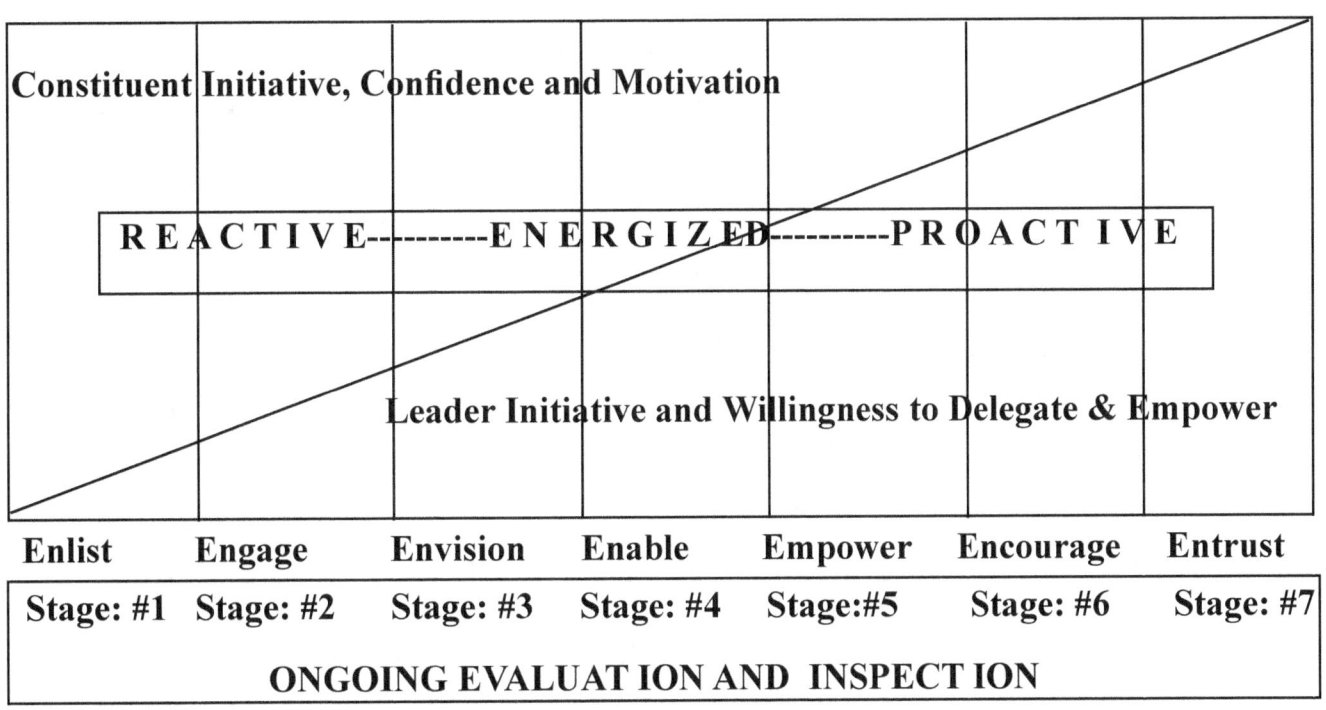

The continuum defines constituent behavior ranging from REACTIVE to ENERGIZED to PROACTIVE. The left-hand portion of the continuum focuses on the degree of ini-tiative, confidence, and motivation demonstrated by the constituent. Whereas, the right-hand portion of the continuum focuses on the degree of leader generated initiative and willingness to delegate and empower constituents. From left to right, the seven stages of individual development and empowerment identified on the continuum are: Stage 1: Enlist, Stage 2: Engage, Stage 3: Envision, Stage 4: En-Encourage, and Stage 7: Entrust.

Developing People... A Team Building Process

Stages of Individual Development & Empowerment

Stage: #1 **Enlist** the individual's support

Stage: #2 **Engage** the individual's interest by addressing the well-known radio station they listen to: WIIFM (What's in it for me!)

Stage: #3 **Envision** a view of a future yet to be...and show them how they are uniquely qualified to contribute to this future.

Stage: #4 **Enable** them to redefine expectations for self and others in order to shape an environment which permits them to contribute to the success of the team.

Stage: #5 **Empower** them by establishing their boundary parameters and provide them with the necessary resources and tools they need for accomplishing results.

Stage: #6 **Encourage** them to go beyond self-imposed expectations, recognize their willingness to think anew and reward their contributions.

Stage: #7 **Entrust** them to take individual responsibility by being "response-able" or "able to respond" to the challenges and opportunities that face them each day.

Summary: It is important for the leader to take the time to focus on the need for **Ongoing Evaluation and Inspection** through the skillful use of effective communication skills such as Listening and Feedback. This approach can be applied during the day to day interactions between Constituent and Leader, as well as through periodic scheduled One-on-One discussions.

How do effective leaders obtain employee involvement and strengthen their teams?

One individual at a time!

Managing Conflict:
Conflict Reaction Questionnaire (CRQ)

Conflict can emerge over anything from personalities and emotions to issues and principles. Half the battle of dealing with conflict constructively comes from understanding the root cause of conflict. Most workplace conflict stems from two root causes: personalities and issues. Take a few moments to respond to the following items:

1. Define conflict in one or two words.

   _____

2. What are the three most important things in your life right now?

   _____

   _____

   _____

3. What would you consider to be a main cause of conflict in your life and/or job?

   _____

4. What steps have you taken to reduce conflict in your life and/or job?

   _____

5. What is your most common reaction to a conflict situation?

   _____

6. How would you like to be able to deal with a conflict situation?

   _____

7. On a scale from one(least) to ten(most) how much conflict has the past week contained? _____

See next page for analysis of your responses

Analysis of Your Responses to Conflict Reaction Questionnaire (CRQ)

Question #1: How you define conflict is the essence of your conflict reaction. What you <u>believe</u> you need, at this time, is actually the <u>opposite</u> of this. In other words, don't focus on what you don't want (the conflict), focus on what you want and need (a sense of power and control). What steps can you take to relieve conflict by reprogramming the belief?

Definition:	**What You Need:**
-uncertainty	-certainty
-overwhelmed	-to take one thing at a time
-frustration	-feeling of adequacy, competency
*feeling of no control	***feeling of control**

Question #2: The most important things in your life have the highest conflict potential. If they weren't so important, you wouldn't care about them as much as you do. As these things are threatened, our feelings of conflict increase.

Question #3: Have the main causes of conflict in your life and/or job been a pattern in your life or are they an isolated incident? What resources might you need to be able to respond to these differently? What are your desired outcomes in these situations and what choices do you have to make them happen?

Question #4: Are the steps that you have taken to reduce conflict in your life working for you? Have you done a realistic assessment of your actions? Are you willing to do something different?

Question #5: Do you become motivated or de-motivated as a result of your common reaction to a conflict situation? Do you tend to confront, avoid, or deny the situation? Do your actions serve to eliminate the conflict, postpone it, or make it worse?

Question #6: Do you know someone (real or fictional) who is able to effectively deal with a conflict situation? Model their behavior. What stops you from doing this? What do you need to do to be able to do this? Create a strategy, ie: setting priorities, identifying actions to create certainty and/or developing skills to enhance your effectiveness.

Question #7: If your score about how conflict ridden the past week has been is between:
- 1-3: What are you doing right?
- 4-6: What needs to be put in balance?
- 7-10: What has gotten out-of-control? Once identified, what steps can be taken to reduce the stress response?

Managing Conflict

Step #1: **Describe the conflict immediately as a "mutual problem."**
"We have a problem. You and I have been...."(describe the problem) OR "I have observed that...."(describe the individual's behavior). "Is that a fair statement of our conflict?"

Step #2: **Offer to Negotiate Differences**
"Can we negotiate this matter? I'd like to find a solution that will work for both of us. Are you willing to try to find one?"

Step #3: **Brainstorm Alternative Solutions Together**
"Let's take turns coming up with ideas on how we can solve this. Would you like to start or do you want me to begin?"

Step #4: **Evaluate the Brainstormed Solutions**
Use these questions to evaluate potential solutions:
- Would it really solve the problem?
- What would be the costs to each party?
- If the solution cannot be included now, can it be put on hold?

Step #5: **Decide on the Best Solution**
Keep in mind that typically one solution may appear to be much better than the rest, but try not to select the first solution without at least evaluating some of the others. Remember, there may be a second right answer!

Step #6: **Plan How the Solution Will Be Implemented**
The negotiation is not complete until each party has committed to a plan for implementation. This step involves thinking through together the questions of who will do what and when.

Step #7: **Follow-Through and Follow-Up**

A designated time in the near future should be agreed upon when both of the parties may evaluate how well the solution is working.

Guiding Change focused on Systematic Inquiry

"Fail, forward, fast" are three words that best-selling business author Tom Peters uses to describe the characteristics of productive, leading-edge, flexible and forward-moving enterprises. We can also learn about change from Greek Philosopher Heraclitus, who said, "the only constant in life is change." As much as this is true, what he did not tell us eons ago was that change has a direction...and it is focused on the future!

The challenge of the constant known as change affects individuals, teams, the workplace and the marketplace. In fact, **change is pervasive** within everything and everybody. What distinguishes both effective individuals and organizations from those who are ineffective is how each one **responds to and manages change.** These individuals and organizations recognize the importance and value of the ability to be responsive to the demands of change. Therefore, how we respond to change determines our ability to succeed or fail. Effective leaders understand the value of **guiding change** by focus-ing on systematic inquiry. **Systematic inquiry** refers to a five-phase problem identifi-cation and problem-solving process which permits individuals and organizations to establish a methodology promoting change through inquiry, interaction, and collabora-tion. These phases are: 1. Assess, 2. Develop/Plan, 3. Implement/Pilot, 4. Measure/ Monitor, and 5. Evaluate. This process is cyclical and focused on continuous improvement.

Guiding Change focused on Systematic Inquiry

Getting Things Done is Change

A primary reason many change efforts fail is that leadership doesn't consider the change from the constituent's perspective. With any change effort, leaders need to address con-cerns people have when they have them. Unless you take the time to meet individual concerns, you won't be able to generate and maintain the momentum necessary for the change to be successful. Consider the following six levels of response and concern from the constituent's perspective as they approach change within themselves, as opposed to change within the organizations.

Constituent's first level of response to proposed change is to ask, "What is it?"

The second level of change addresses the concern "How will it personally affect me?" (What's in it for me?) This is the most overlooked and undermanaged concern in the change process and for these reasons, why most changes fail. People affected by a pending change have a host of questions they need answered in order to feel safe: "How will the change affect me and my role (job)?" "Will I still have a role (job)?" "Will this require more time or effort on my part?" "How will I be evaluated regarding this change?" and so forth.

Level three addresses the pragmatic question of "How will this change be conducted?"

Level four is the level that leadership typically starts with when they announce a change; that is, the benefits to the company.

Level five is the level of the true believer—that person who has experienced the change and comes to appreciate that the benefits of the change exceed the effort and problems encountered in making it happen. These individuals become committed to fully imple-menting the change.

In the final level of concern, the individual looks beyond the intended change for new and related ways to innovate."

> Change is a constant throughout life, and how we adapt to change determines whether we grow and evolve as individuals, or whether we become stagnant and inflexible.

Where Do You Go From Here?
Applying the Seven Basic Leadership Principles

Best of Luck as You Continue Your LeaderSELF Journey...

1. Focus on the specific situation, issue or behavior, not on the person. Whether one is talking about child-rearing or leadership, this principle is key to one's effectiveness in interacting with others. By using this principle, one build's rapport and avoids defensive and uncooperative behavior. This principle is important to keep in mind, whether one is providing another with praise or criticism.

2. Demonstrate trust and respect in order to support the self-confidence and self-esteem of others. Relationships at home and at work are built upon trust and respect. Take the time to treat others *the way they want to be treated* in order to build their self-confidence and self-esteem.

3. Strengthen cooperative and constructive relationships with others.
Healthy relationships reduce stress and increase morale which strengthens interdependent work relationships.

4. Never underestimate the power of effective communication and teamwork.
Two-way communication and teamwork go hand-in-hand. Communication and teamwork are essential to success for all high performing sports and organizational teams.

5. Lead by example and take initiative to make things happen.
"Just Do It!" By taking initiative and leading by example you are able to demonstrate to others in your organization what is important to you. This behavior encourages others to emulate your actions.

6. Obtain the information first, by asking "What Happened?"
In order to make proper decisions, an individual needs to understand a situation "from the other person's perspective." By asking "What Happened?" an individual creates a non-judgemental environment for obtaining the information they need.

7. Understand why personal styles and preferences require behavioral flexibility.
As human beings, we share one thing in common. We are all unique! Understanding the personal styles and preferences of ourselves and others provides us with the ability to adjust our style and preference to "match" that of another. As a result of this behavioral flexibility, we allow an individual to remain in their comfort zone. And when comfort levels increase, so does their ability to cooperate.

Recommended "Classic" Leadership Books

Anderson, E. (2002). Strengthsquest. Discover and develop your strengths in academics and beyond. The Gallup Organization. Washington, D.C.

Blanchard, K. & Bowles, S. (2001). *High Five!* New York, NY: William Morrow.

Bateman, Snell (2007). Management: Leading and Collaborating. 7th Edition. ISBN: 13: 978-0-07-292330-8 10: 0-07-292330-X

Blanchard, K. & Hersey, P. (1982). *Management of Organizational Behavior.* Englewood Cliffs, NJ: Prentice-Hall..

Bolman, L.G. & Deal, T.E. (1997). *Reframing Organizations* (pp. 14-248). San Francisco: Jossey Bass.

Bolman, L. G., & Deal, T. E. (2001). *Leading with Soul*. San Francisco, CA: Jossey-Bass.

Buckingham, M. & Coffman, C. (1999). First, Break All the Rules. New York, NY: Simon and Schuster.

Clifton, D. & Buckingham, M. (2001). Now, Discover Your Strengths. New York, NY: The Free Press.

Clifton, D. How Full is Your Bucket? NY, NY: Gallup Press. ISBN: 1595620036

Cooper, R. & Sawaf, A. (1997). Executive EQ. emotional intelligence in leadership and organizations. New York, NY: Grosset/Putnam.

Covey, S.R. (1990). Seven Habits of Highly Effective People. New York, NY: Simon and Schuster.

Goleman, D. (1995). Emotional Intelligence. why it can matter more than IQ. New York, NY: Ban-tam Books.

Goleman, D. (1998). Working With Emotional Intelligence ISBN: 0553378589

Goleman, D. (2002). Primal Leadership. realizing the power of emotional intelligence. Boston, MA: Harvard University Press.

Kotter, J. P. (1990, May-June). What Leaders Really Do. Harvard Business Review, 246-258.

Kouzes, J. M., & Posner, B. Z. (1987). *The Leadership Challenge*. San Francisco,CA: Jossey- Bass.

Light, R. (2001). Making the Most of College: Students Speak Their Minds. Cambridge, MA: Harvard University Press.

Ornish, D. (1998). Love and Survival. New York, NY: Harper Collins.

Phillips, D. (1992). Lincoln on Leadership. Warner books. ISBN: 0446394599